Los Angeles Angels 2021

A Baseball Companion

Edited by Steven Goldman and Bret Sayre

Baseball Prospectus

Craig Brown, Associate Editor
Robert Au, Harry Pavlidis and Amy Pircher, Statistics Editors

Copyright © 2021 by DIY Baseball, LLC.
All rights reserved

This book or any part thereof may not be reproduced or transmitted in any form or by any means, electronic or mechanical, including photocopying, recording, or by any information storage and retrieval system, without permission in writing from the publisher.

Limit of Liability/Disclaimer of Warranty: While the publisher and the author have used their best efforts in preparing this book, they make no representations or warranties with respect to the accuracy or completeness of the contents of this book and specifically disclaim any implied warranties of merchantability or fitness for a particular purpose. No warranty may be created or extended by sales representatives or written sales materials. The advice and strategies contained herein may not be suitable for your situation. You should consult with a professional where appropriate. Neither the publisher nor the author shall be liable for any loss of profit or any other commercial damages, including but not limited to special, incidental, consequential, or other damages.

Library of Congress Cataloging-in-Publication Data:
paperback
ISBN-13: 978-1-950716-49-4

Project Credits
Cover Design: Ginny Searle
Interior Design and Production: Amy Pircher, Robert Au
Layout: Amy Pircher, Robert Au

Baseball icon courtesy of Uberux, from https://www.shareicon.net/author/uberux

Ballpark diagram courtesy of Lou Spirito/THIRTY81 Project, https://thirty81project.com/

Manufactured in the United States of America
10 9 8 7 6 5 4 3 2 1

Table of Contents

Statistical Introduction v

Part 1: Team Analysis

Performance Graphs 3
2020 Team Performance 4
2021 Team Projections 5
Team Personnel 6
Angel Stadium Stats 7
Angels Team Analysis 9

Part 2: Player Analysis

Angels Player Analysis 16
Angels Prospects 91

Part 3: Featured Articles

Angels All-Time Top 10 Players 103
    by Matthew Trueblood

A Taxonomy of 2020 Abnormalities 109
    by Rob Mains

Tranches of WAR 115
    by Russell A. Carleton

Secondhand Sport 121
    by Patrick Dubuque

Steve Dalkowski Dreaming 125
    by Steven Goldman

A Reward For A Functioning Society 129
    by Cory Frontin and Craig Goldstein

Index of Names 133

Statistical Introduction

Sports are, fundamentally, a blend of athletic endeavor and storytelling. Baseball, like any other sport, tells its stories in so many ways: in the arc of a game from the stands or a season from the box scores, in photos, or even in numbers. At Baseball Prospectus, we understand that statistics don't replace observation or any of baseball's stories, but complement everything else that makes the game so much fun.

What stats help us with is with patterns and precision, variance and value. This book can help you learn things you may not see from watching a game or hundred, whether it's the path of a career over time or the breadth of the entire MLB. We'd also never ask you to choose between our numbers and the experience of viewing a game from the cheap seats or the comfort of your home; our publication combines running the numbers with observations and wisdom from some of the brightest minds we can find. But if you *do* want to learn more about the numbers beyond what's on the backs of player jerseys, let us help explain.

Offense

We've revised our methodology for determining batting value. Long-time readers of the book will notice that we've retired True Average in favor of a new metric: Deserved Runs Created Plus (DRC+). Developed by Jonathan Judge and our stats team, this statistic measures everything a player does at the plate–reaching base, hitting for power, making outs, and moving runners over–and puts it on a scale where 100 equals league-average performance. A DRC+ of 150 is terrific, a DRC+ of 100 is average and a DRC+ of 75 means you better be an excellent defender.

DRC+ also does a better job than any of our previous metrics in taking contextual factors into account. The model adjusts for how the park affects performance, but also for things like the talent of the opposing pitcher, value of different types of batted-ball events, league, temperature and other factors. It's able to describe a player's expected offensive contribution than any other statistic we've found over the years, and also does a better job of predicting future performance as well.

The other aspect of run-scoring is baserunning, which we quantify using Baserunning Runs. BRR not only records the value of stolen bases (or getting caught in the act), but also accounts for all the stuff that doesn't show up on the back of a baseball card: a runner's ability to go first to third on a single, or advance on a fly ball.

Defense

Where offensive value is *relatively* easy to identify and understand, defensive value is … not. Over the past dozen years, the sabermetric community has focused mostly on stats based on zone data: a real-live human person records the type of batted ball and estimated landing location, and models are created that give expected outs. From there, you can compare fielders' actual outs to those expected ones. Simple, right?

Unfortunately, zone data has two major issues. First, zone data is recorded by commercial data providers who keep the raw data private unless you pay for it. (All the statistics we build in this book and on our website use public data as inputs.) That hurts our ability to test assumptions or duplicate results. Second, over the years it has become apparent that there's quite a bit of "noise" in zone-based fielding analysis. Sometimes the conclusions drawn from zone data don't hold up to scrutiny, and sometimes the different data provided by different providers don't look anything alike, giving wildly different results. Sometimes the hard-working professional stringers or scorers might unknowingly inflict unconscious bias into the mix: for example good fielders will often be credited with more expected outs despite the data, and ballparks with high press boxes tend to score more line drives than ones with a lower press box.

Enter our Fielding Runs Above Average (FRAA). For most positions, FRAA is built from play-by-play data, which allows us to avoid the subjectivity found in many other fielding metrics. The idea is this: count how many fielding plays are made by a given player and compare that to expected plays for an average fielder at their position (based on pitcher ground ball tendencies and batter handedness). Then we adjust for park and base-out situations.

When it comes to catchers, our methodology is a little different thanks to the laundry list of responsibilities they're tasked with beyond just, well, catching and throwing the ball. By now you've probably heard about "framing" or the art of making umpires more likely to call balls outside the strike zone for strikes. To put this into one tidy number, we incorporate pitch tracking data (for the years it exists) and adjust for important factors like pitcher, umpire, batter and home-field advantage using a mixed-model approach. This grants us a number for how many strikes the catcher is personally adding to (or subtracting from) his pitchers' performance … which we then convert to runs added or lost using linear weights.

Framing is one of the biggest parts of determining catcher value, but we also take into account blocking balls from going past, whether a scorer deems it a passed ball or a wild pitch. We use a similar approach—one that really benefits from the pitch tracking data that tells us what ends up in the dirt and what doesn't. We also include a catcher's ability to prevent stolen bases and how well they field balls in play, and *finally* we come up with our FRAA for catchers.

Pitching

Both pitching and fielding make up the half of baseball that isn't run scoring: run prevention. Separating pitching from fielding is a tough task, and most recent pitching analysis has branched off from Voros McCracken's famous (and controversial) statement, "There is little if any difference among major-league pitchers in their ability to prevent hits on balls hit in the field of play." The research of the analytic community has validated this to some extent, and there are a host of "defense-independent" pitching measures that have been developed to try and extract the effect of the defense behind a hurler from the pitcher's work.

Our solution to this quandary is Deserved Run Average (DRA), our core pitching metric. DRA seeks to evaluate a pitcher's performance, much like earned run average (ERA), the tried-and-true pitching stat you've seen on every baseball broadcast or box score from the past century, but it's very different. To start, DRA takes an event-by-event look at what the pitchers does, and adjusts the value of that event based on different environmental factors like park, batter, catcher, umpire, base-out situation, run differential, inning, defense, home field advantage, pitcher role and temperature. That mixed model gives us a pitcher's expected contribution, similar to what we do for our DRC+ model for hitters and FRAA model for catchers. (Oh, and we also consider the pitcher's effect on basestealing and on balls getting past the catcher.)

DRA is set to the scale of runs allowed per nine innings (RA9) instead of ERA, which makes DRA's scale slightly higher than ERA's. Because of this, for ease of use, we're supplying DRA-, which is much easier for the reader to parse. As with DRC+, DRA- is an "index" stat, meaning instead of using some arbitrary and shifting number to denote what's "good," average is always 100. The reason that it uses a minus rather than a plus is because like ERA, a lower number is better. Therefore a 75 DRA- describes a performance 25 percent better than average, whereas a 150 DRA- means that either a pitcher is getting extremely lucky with their results, or getting ready to try a new pitch.

Since the last time you picked up an edition of this book, we've also made a few minor changes to DRA to make it better. Recent research into "tunneling"—the act of throwing consecutive pitches that appear similar from a batter's point of view until after the swing decision point–data has given us a new contextual factor to account for in DRA: plate distance. This refers to the distance between successive pitches as they approach the plate, and while it has a smaller effect than factors like velocity or whiff rate, it still can help explain pitcher strikeout rate in our model.

Recently Added Descriptive Statistics

Returning to our 2021 edition of the book are a few figures which recently appeared. These numbers may be a little bit more familiar to those of you who have spent some time investigating baseball statistics.

Fastball Percentage

Our fastball percentage (FA%) statistic measures how frequently a pitcher throws a pitch classified as a "fastball," measured as a percentage of overall pitches thrown. We qualify three types of fastballs:

1. The traditional four-seam fastball;
2. The two-seam fastball or sinker;
3. "Hard cutters," which are pitches that have the movement profile of a cut fastball and are used as the pitcher's primary offering or in place of a more traditional fastball.

For example, a pitcher with a FA% of 67 throws any combination of these three pitches about two-thirds of the time.

Whiff Rate

Everybody loves a swing and a miss, and whiff rate (Whiff%) measures how frequently pitchers induce a swinging strike. To calculate Whiff%, we add up all the pitches thrown that ended with a swinging strike, then divide that number by a pitcher's total pitches thrown. Most often, high whiff rates correlate with high strikeout rates (and overall effective pitcher performance).

Called Strike Probability

Called Strike Probability (CSP) is a number that represents the likelihood that all of a pitcher's pitches will be called a strike while controlling for location, pitcher and batter handedness, umpire and count. Here's how it works: on each pitch, our model determines how many times (out of 100) that a similar pitch was called for a strike given those factors mentioned above, and when normalized for each batter's strike zone. Then we average the CSP for all pitches thrown by a pitcher in a season, and that gives us the yearly CSP percentage you see in the stats boxes.

As you might imagine, pitchers with a higher CSP are more likely to work in the zone, where pitchers with a lower CSP are likely locating their pitches outside the normal strike zone, for better or for worse.

Projections

Many of you aren't turning to this book just for a look at what a player has done, but for a look at what a player is going to do: the PECOTA projections. PECOTA, initially developed by Nate Silver (who has moved on to greater fame as a political analyst), consists of three parts:

1. Major-league equivalencies, which use minor-league statistics to project how a player will perform in the major leagues;
2. Baseline forecasts, which use weighted averages and regression to the mean to estimate a player's current true talent level; and
3. Aging curves, which uses the career paths of comparable players to estimate how a player's statistics are likely to change over time.

With all those important things covered, let's take a look at what's in the book this year.

Team Prospectus

Most of this book is composed of team chapters, with one for each of the 30 major-league franchises. On the first page of each chapter, you'll see a box that contains some of the key statistics for each team as well as a very inviting stadium diagram.

We start with the team name, their unadjusted 2020 win-loss record, and their divisional ranking. Beneath that are a host of other team statistics. **Pythag** presents an adjusted 2020 winning percentage, calculated by taking runs scored per game (**RS/G**) and runs allowed per game (**RA/G**) for the team, and running them through a version of Bill James' Pythagorean formula that was refined and improved by David Smyth and Brandon Heipp. (The formula is called "Pythagenpat," which is equally fun to type and to say.)

Next up is **DRC+**, described earlier, to indicate the overall hitting ability of the team either above or below league-average. Run prevention on the pitching side is covered by **DRA** (also mentioned earlier) and another metric: Fielding Independent Pitching (**FIP**), which calculates another ERA-like statistic based on strikeouts, walks, and home runs recorded. Defensive Efficiency Rating (**DER**) tells us the percentage of balls in play turned into outs for the team, and is a quick fielding shorthand that rounds out run prevention.

After that, we have several measures related to roster composition, as opposed to on-field performance. **B-Age** and **P-Age** tell us the average age of a team's batters and pitchers, respectively. **Payroll** is the combined team payroll for all on-field players, and Doug Pappas' Marginal Dollars per Marginal Win (**M$/MW**) tells us how much money a team spent to earn production above replacement level.

Next to each of these stats, we've listed each team's MLB rank in that category from first to 30th. In this, first always indicates a positive outcome and 30th a negative outcome, except in the case of salary—first is highest.

After the franchise statistics, we share a few items about the team's home ballpark. There's the aforementioned diagram of the park's dimensions (including distances to the outfield wall), a graphic showing the height of the wall from the left-field pole to the right-field pole, and a table showing three-year park factors for the stadium. The park factors are displayed as indexes where 100 is average, 110 means that the park inflates the statistic in question by 10 percent, and 90 means that the park deflates the statistic in question by 10 percent.

On the second page of each team chapter, you'll find three graphs. The first is **Payroll History** and helps you see how the team's payroll has compared to the MLB and divisional average payrolls over time. Payroll figures are current as of January 1, 2021; with so many free agents still unsigned as of this writing, the final 2021 figure will likely be significantly different for many teams. (In the meantime, you can always find the most current data at Baseball Prospectus' Cot's Baseball Contracts page.)

The second graph is **Future Commitments** and helps you see the team's future outlays, if any.

The third graph is **Farm System Ranking** and displays how the Baseball Prospectus prospect team has ranked the organization's farm system since 2007.

After the graphs, we have a **Personnel** section that lists many of the important decision-makers and upper-level field and operations staff members for the franchise, as well as any former Baseball Prospectus staff members who are currently part of the organization. (In very rare circumstances, someone might be on both lists!)

Position Players

After all that information and a thoughtful bylined essay covering each team, we present our player comments. These are also bylined, but due to frequent franchise shifts during the offseason, our bylines are more a rough guide than a perfect accounting of who wrote what.

Each player is listed with the major-league team that employed him as of early January 2021. If a player changed teams after that point via free agency, trade, or any other method, you'll be able to find them in the chapter for their previous squad.

As an example, take a look at the player comment for Padres shortstop Fernando Tatis Jr.: the stat block that accompanies his written comment is at the top of this page. First we cover biographical information (age is as of June 30, 2021) before moving onto the stats themselves. Our statistic columns include standard identifying information like **YEAR**, **TEAM**, **LVL** (level of affiliated play) and **AGE** before getting into the numbers. Next, we provide raw, untranslated

Fernando Tatis Jr.   SS
Born: 01/02/99   Age: 22   Bats: R   Throws: R
Height: 6'3"   Weight: 217   Origin: International Free Agent, 2015

YEAR	TEAM	LVL	AGE	PA	R	2B	3B	HR	RBI	BB	K	SB	CS	AVG/OBP/SLG
2018	SA	AA	19	394	77	22	4	16	43	33	109	16	5	.286/.355/.507
2019	SD	MLB	20	372	61	13	6	22	53	30	110	16	6	.317/.379/.590
2020	SD	MLB	21	257	50	11	2	17	45	27	61	11	3	.277/.366/.571
2021 FS	SD	MLB	22	600	95	24	4	31	81	50	165	17	8	.263/.331/.499
2021 DC	SD	MLB	22	628	100	25	4	32	85	53	173	19	8	.263/.331/.499

Comparables: Darryl Strawberry, Bo Bichette, Ronald Acuña Jr.

YEAR	TEAM	LVL	AGE	PA	DRC+	BABIP	BRR	FRAA	WARP
2018	SA	AA	19	394	136	.370	3.0	SS(83): -1.9	2.4
2019	SD	MLB	20	372	118	.410	7.1	SS(83): 0.9	3.4
2020	SD	MLB	21	257	126	.306	0.7	SS(57): -5.5	0.9
2021 FS	SD	MLB	22	600	126	.318	1.7	SS -1	3.9
2021 DC	SD	MLB	22	628	126	.318	1.8	SS -1	4.0

numbers like you might find on the back of your dad's baseball cards: **PA** (plate appearances), **R** (runs), **2B** (doubles), **3B** (triples), **HR** (home runs), **RBI** (runs batted in), **BB** (walks), **K** (strikeouts), **SB** (stolen bases) and **CS** (caught stealing).

Following the basic stats is **Whiff%** (whiff rate), which denotes how often, when a batter swings, he fails to make contact with the ball. Another way to think of this number is an inverse of a hitter's contact rate.

Next, we have unadjusted "slash" statistics: **AVG** (batting average), **OBP** (on-base percentage) and **SLG** (slugging percentage). Following the slash line is **DRC+** (Deserved Runs Created Plus), which we described earlier as total offensive expected contribution compared to the league average.

BABIP (batting average on balls in play) tells us how often a ball in play fell for a hit, and can help us identify whether a batter may have been lucky or not ... but note that high BABIPs also tend to follow the great hitters of our time, as well as speedy singles hitters who put the ball on the ground.

The next item is **BRR** (Baserunning Runs), which covers all of a player's baserunning accomplishments including (but not limited to) swiped bags and failed attempts. Next is **FRAA** (Fielding Runs Above Average), which also includes the number of games previously played at each position noted in parentheses. Multi-position players have only their two most frequent positions listed here, but their total FRAA number reflects all positions played.

Our last column here is **WARP** (Wins Above Replacement Player). WARP estimates the total value of a player, which means for hitters it takes into account hitting runs above average (calculated using the DRC+ model), BRR and FRAA. Then, it makes an adjustment for positions played and gives the player a credit

Los Angeles Angels 2021

for plate appearances based upon the difference between "replacement level"—which is derived from the quality of players added to a team's roster after the start of the season–and the league average.

The final line just below the stats box is **PECOTA** data, which is discussed further in a following section.

Catchers

Catchers are a special breed, and thus they have earned their own separate box which displays some of the defensive metrics that we've built just for them. As an example, let's check out Yasmani Grandal.

YEAR	TEAM	P. COUNT	FRM RUNS	BLK RUNS	THRW RUNS	TOT RUNS
2018	LAD	16816	15.7	0.8	0.1	16.5
2019	MIL	18740	19.4	1.8	-0.1	21.1
2020	CHW	4830	3.7	0.3	-0.2	3.8
2021	CHW	14430	16.7	-0.6	1.0	17.1
2021	CHW	14430	16.7	0.4	1.0	18.0

The **YEAR** and **TEAM** columns match what you'd find in the other stat box. **P. COUNT** indicates the number of pitches thrown while the catcher was behind the plate, including swinging strikes, fouls and balls in play. **FRM RUNS** is the total run value the catcher provided (or cost) his team by influencing the umpire to call strikes where other catchers did not. **BLK RUNS** expresses the total run value above or below average for the catcher's ability to prevent wild pitches and passed balls. **THRW RUNS** is calculated using a similar model as the previous two statistics, and it measures a catcher's ability to throw out basestealers but also to dissuade them from testing his arm in the first place. It takes into account factors like the pitcher (including his delivery and pickoff move) and baserunner (who could be as fast as Billy Hamilton or as slow as Yonder Alonso). **TOT RUNS** is the sum of all of the previous three statistics.

Pitchers

Let's give our pitchers a turn, using 2020 AL Cy Young winner Shane Bieber as our example. Take a look at his stat block: the first line and the **YEAR**, **TEAM**, **LVL** and **AGE** columns are the same as in the position player example earlier.

Here too, we have a series of columns that display raw, unadjusted statistics compiled by the pitcher over the course of a season: **W** (wins), **L** (losses), **SV** (saves), **G** (games pitched), **GS** (games started), **IP** (innings pitched), **H** (hits allowed) and **HR** (home runs allowed). Next we have two statistics that are rates: **BB/9** (walks per nine innings) and **K/9** (strikeouts per nine innings), before returning to the unadjusted K (strikeouts).

Next up is **GB%** (ground ball percentage), which is the percentage of all batted balls that were hit on the ground, including both outs and hits. Remember, this is based on observational data and subject to human error, so please approach this with a healthy dose of skepticism.

BABIP (batting average on balls in play) is calculated using the same methodology as it is for position players, but it often tells us more about a pitcher than it does a hitter. With pitchers, a high BABIP is often due to poor defense or bad luck, and can often be an indicator of potential rebound, and a low BABIP may be cause to expect performance regression. (A typical league-average BABIP is close to .290-.300.)

The metrics **WHIP** (walks plus hits per inning pitched) and **ERA** (earned run average) are old standbys: WHIP measures walks and hits allowed on a per-inning basis, while ERA measures earned runs on a nine-inning basis. Neither of these stats are translated or adjusted.

DRA- (Deserved Run Average) was described at length earlier, and measures how the pitcher "deserved" to perform compared to other pitchers. Please note that since we lack all the data points that would make for a "real" DRA for minor-league events, the DRA- displayed for minor league partial-seasons is based off of different data. (That data is a modified version of our cFIP metric, which you can find more information about on our website.)

Shane Bieber   RHP

Born: 05/31/95   Age: 26   Bats: R   Throws: R
Height: 6'3"   Weight: 200   Origin: Round 4, 2016 Draft (#122 overall)

YEAR	TEAM	LVL	AGE	W	L	SV	G	GS	IP	H	HR	BB/9	K/9	K	GB%	BABIP
2018	AKR	AA	23	3	0	0	5	5	31	26	1	0.3	8.7	30	47.3%	.278
2018	COL	AAA	23	3	1	0	8	8	48²	30	3	1.1	8.7	47	52.0%	.227
2018	CLE	MLB	23	11	5	0	20	19	114²	130	13	1.8	9.3	118	46.2%	.356
2019	CLE	MLB	24	15	8	0	34	33	214¹	186	31	1.7	10.9	259	44.4%	.298
2020	CLE	MLB	25	8	1	0	12	12	77¹	46	7	2.4	14.2	122	48.4%	.267
2021 FS	CLE	MLB	26	10	6	0	26	26	150	121	18	2.1	11.7	195	45.5%	.297
2021 DC	CLE	MLB	26	14	7	0	30	30	196.7	159	24	2.1	11.7	257	45.5%	.297

Comparables: Luis Severino, Danny Salazar, Joe Musgrove

YEAR	TEAM	LVL	AGE	WHIP	ERA	DRA-	WARP	MPH	FB%	WHF	CSP
2018	AKR	AA	23	0.87	1.16	61	0.9				
2018	COL	AAA	23	0.74	1.66	69	1.2				
2018	CLE	MLB	23	1.33	4.55	74	2.6	94.7	57.4%	26.2%	
2019	CLE	MLB	24	1.05	3.28	75	4.9	94.4	45.8%	30.8%	
2020	CLE	MLB	25	0.87	1.63	53	2.6	95.3	53.6%	40.7%	
2021 FS	CLE	MLB	26	1.04	2.44	64	4.4	94.7	50.0%	33.2%	44.2%
2021 DC	CLE	MLB	26	1.04	2.44	64	5.8	94.7	50.0%	33.2%	44.2%

Just like with hitters, **WARP** (Wins Above Replacement Player) is a total value metric that puts pitchers of all stripes on the same scale as position players. We use DRA as the primary input for our calculation of WARP. You might notice that relief pitchers (due to their limited innings) may have a lower WARP than you were expecting or than you might see in other WARP-like metrics. WARP does not take leverage into account, just the actions a pitcher performs and the expected value of those actions ... which ends up judging high-leverage relief pitchers differently than you might imagine given their prestige and market value.

MPH gives you the pitcher's 95th percentile velocity for the noted season, in order to give you an idea of what the *peak* fastball velocity a pitcher possesses. Since this comes from our pitch-tracking data, it is not publicly available for minor-league pitchers.

Finally, we display the three new pitching metrics we described earlier. **FB%** (fastball percentage) gives you the percentage of fastballs thrown out of all pitches. **WHF** (whiff rate) tells you the percentage of swinging strikes induced out of all pitches. **CSP** (called strike probability) expresses the likelihood of all pitches thrown to result in a called strike, after controlling for factors like handedness, umpire, pitch type, count and location.

PECOTA

All players have PECOTA projections for 2021, as well as a set of other numbers that describe the performance of comparable players according to PECOTA. All projections for 2021 are for the player at the date we went to press in early January and are projected into the league and park context as indicated by the team abbreviation. (Note that players at very low levels of the minors are too unpredictable to assess using these numbers.) All PECOTA projected statistics represent a player's projected major-league performance.

How we're doing that is a little different this season. There are really two different values that go into the final stat line that you see for PECOTA: How a player performs, and how much playing time he'll be given to perform it. In the past we've estimated playing time based on each team's roster and depth charts, and we'll continue to do that. These projections are denoted as **2021 DC**.

But in many cases, a player won't be projected for major-league playing time; most of the time this is because they aren't projected to be major-league players at all, but still developing as prospects. Or perhaps a player will provide Triple-A depth, only to have an opportunity open up because of injury. For these purposes, we're also supplying a second projection, labeled **2021 FS**, or full season. This is what we would project the player to provide in 600 plate appearances or 150 innings pitched.

Below the projections are the player's three highest-scoring comparable players as determined by PECOTA. All comparables represent a snapshot of how the listed player was performing at the same age as the current player, so if a

23-year-old pitcher is compared to Bartolo Colón, he's actually being compared to a 23-year-old Colón, not the version that pitched for the Rangers in 2018, nor to Colón's career as a whole.

A few points about pitcher projections. First, we aren't yet projecting peak velocity, so that column will be blank in the PECOTA lines. Second, projecting DRA is trickier than evaluating past performance, because it is unclear how deserving each pitcher will be of his anticipated outcomes. However, we know that another DRA-related statistic–contextual FIP or cFIP-estimates future run scoring very well. So for PECOTA, the projected DRA- figures you see are based on the past cFIPs generated by the pitcher and comparable players over time, along with the other factors described above.

If you're familiar with PECOTA, then you'll have noticed that the projection system often appears bullish on players coming off a bad year and bearish on players coming off a good year. (This is because the system weights several previous seasons, not just the most recent one.) In addition, we publish the 50th percentile projections for each player–which is smack in the middle of the range of projected production—which tends to mean PECOTA stat lines don't often have extreme results like 40 home runs or 250 strikeouts in a given season. In essence, PECOTA doesn't project very many extreme seasons.

Managers

After all those wonderful team chapters, we've got statistics for each big-league manager, all of whom are organized by alphabetical order. Here you'll find a block including an extraordinary amount of information collected from each manager's entire career. For more information on the acronyms and what they mean, please visit the Glossary at www.baseballprospectus.com.

There is one important metric that we'd like to call attention to, and you'll find it next to each manager's name: **wRM+** (weighted reliever management plus). Developed by Rob Arthur and Rian Watt, wRM+ investigates how good a manager is at using their best relievers during the moments of highest leverage, using both our proprietary DRA metric as well as Leverage Index. wRM+ is scaled to a league average of 100, and a wRM+ of 105 indicates that relievers were used approximately five percent "better" than average. On the other hand, a wRM+ of 95 would tell us the team used its relievers five percent "worse" than the average team.

While wRM+ does not have an extremely strong correlation with a manager, it is statistically significant; this means that a manager is not *entirely* responsible for a team's wRM+, but does have some effect on that number.

Part 1: Team Analysis

Performance Graphs

Payroll History (in millions)

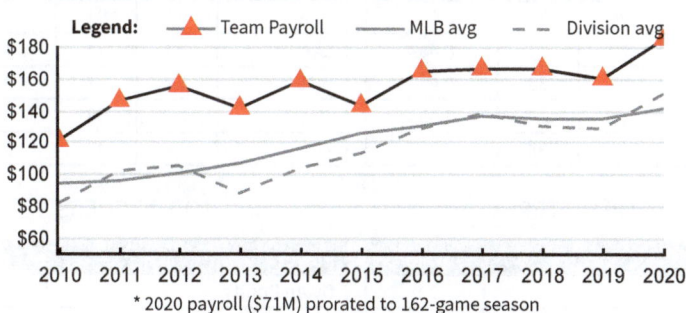

* 2020 payroll ($71M) prorated to 162-game season

Future Commitments (in millions)

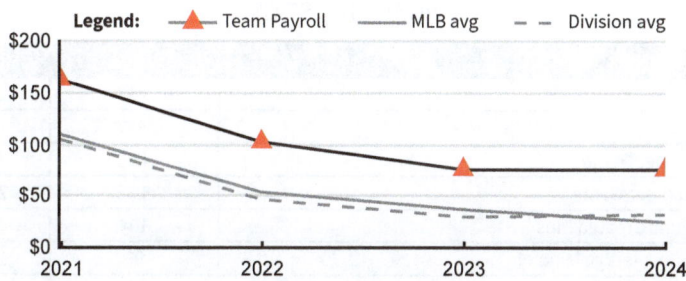

Farm System Ranking

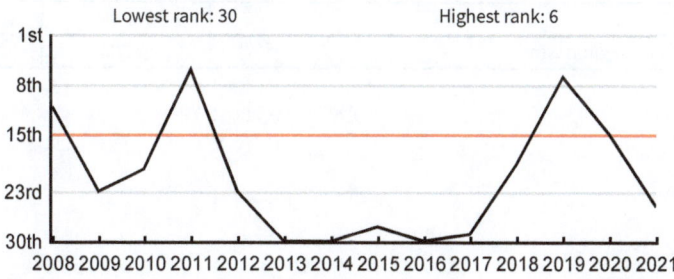

2020 Team Performance

ACTUAL STANDINGS

Team	W	L	Pct
OAK	36	24	0.600
HOU	29	31	0.483
SEA	27	33	0.450
LAA	**26**	**34**	**0.433**
TEX	22	38	0.367

dWIN% STANDINGS

Team	W	L	Pct
OAK	29	31	0.499
LAA	**29**	**31**	**0.497**
HOU	28	32	0.472
SEA	22	38	0.370
TEX	18	42	0.304

TOP HITTERS

Player	WARP
Mike Trout	1.9
Anthony Rendon	0.9
Max Stassi	0.9

TOP PITCHERS

Player	WARP
Dylan Bundy	1.4
Andrew Heaney	1.0
Mike Mayers	0.7

VITAL STATISTICS

Statistic Name	Value	Rank
Pythagenpat	.457	21st
dWin%	.497	11th
Runs Scored per Game	4.90	9th
Runs Allowed per Game	5.35	27th
Deserved Runs Created Plus	104	7th
Deserved Run Average Minus	99	16th
Fielding Independent Pitching	4.52	17th
Defensive Efficiency Rating	.699	17th
Batter Age	29.1	29th
Pitcher Age	27.7	9th
Payroll	$71.0M	7th
Marginal $ per Marginal Win	$6.7M	27th

2021 Team Projections

PROJECTED STANDINGS

Team	W	L	Pct	+/-
HOU	92.5	69.5	0.571	14
There's reason to be skeptical of the starting pitching depth, but this team will score plenty of runs.				
LAA	86.2	75.8	0.532	16
Still buying pitching from the bargain bin despite a new GM, they lack the depth to be great, but if the stars stay healthy, they'll be good.				
OAK	82.2	79.8	0.507	-15
Free-agent departures in the outfield, infield, and bullpen leave them scrambling for coverage despite Matts Chapman and Olson.				
SEA	70.7	91.3	0.436	-2
The rebuild should be nearly over, but will go on for at least another year after a shockingly silent winter.				
TEX	66.8	95.2	0.412	7
A team in total, chaotic transition, but the kids could be fun to watch.				

TOP PROJECTED HITTERS

Player	WARP
Mike Trout	7.5
Anthony Rendon	3.9
Justin Upton	2.1

TOP PROJECTED PITCHERS

Player	WARP
Dylan Bundy	2.9
Andrew Heaney	2.1
José Quintana	1.9

FARM SYSTEM REPORT

Top Prospect	Number of Top 101 Prospects
Brandon Marsh, #44	3

KEY DEDUCTIONS

Player	WARP
Matt Andriese	1.2
Hansel Robles	0.4

KEY ADDITIONS

Player	WARP
José Quintana	1.9
José Iglesias	1.2
Raisel Iglesias	1.0
Alex Cobb	0.8
Dexter Fowler	0.6
Alex Claudio	0.4
Kurt Suzuki	0.3
Aaron Slegers	0.3

Team Personnel

General Manager
Perry Minasian

Assistant General Manager
Alex Tamin

Director, Baseball Operations
Andrew Ball

Manager
Joe Maddon

Angel Stadium Stats

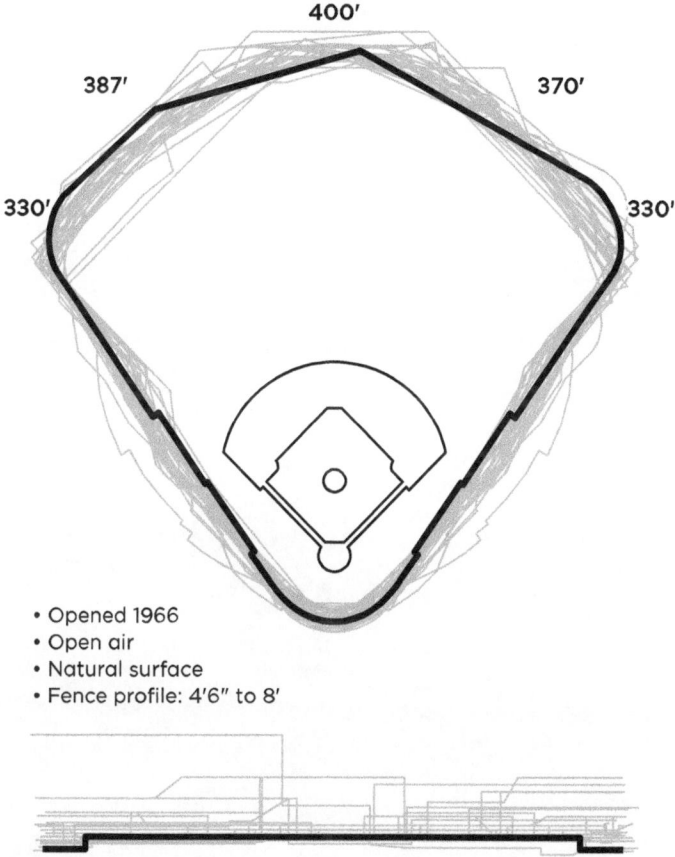

- Opened 1966
- Open air
- Natural surface
- Fence profile: 4'6" to 8'

Three-Year Park Factors

Runs	Runs/RH	Runs/LH	HR/RH	HR/LH
98	98	100	101	107

Angels Team Analysis

In this moment of crudity and avarice and shameless unrepentant bad faith, in the unnerving context of society's most powerful concerns no longer even bothering to act as if they're bound by norms or rules or laws, while being spun through innumerable concurrent crises, it is natural and understandable to wish that your favorite baseball team might be run like a humble family business. If you want to be a jerk about it, it is true that the Gambinos and the Sacklers and the Falwells are also family businesses, but not every family enterprise is quite as gnarled or brutal as the big ones everywhere squeezing and bilking and immiserating the rest of humanity. There are other such businesses that really do resemble the revered American ideal, and which exist as literal brick-and-mortar manifestations of the human drive to provide and succeed and create.

That last bit is the family business dream as it is sold, mostly, although the gilded goblins squatting atop everything cast a cold and ironic shadow over that sentimental concept. But fans who have felt that wish—those on the wrong end of sudden executive austerity, or lost in some ill-defined and quite possibly endless rebuild—know what it's about, which is finally nothing more or less than sensing a human face and some identifiable human motivations behind the behavior of the team to which they have committed some objectively unwise chunk of emotional wellbeing. It's a bad idea to put the happiness of some (or really any) months of your life in the hands of a damn baseball team, but no one who cares about the Angels, or any other baseball team, got into it because it seemed like the savvy thing to do. The salient question, where the uniquely blessed and persistently cursed Angels are concerned, is why and how all that caring came to feel like such a waste.

There are many worse teams and let's say several more dysfunctional organizations than the Angels. Some of the former are quite clearly not trying to be anything at all beyond Recipients Of Profit-Sharing Distributions and the monies owed them in television deals; others are actively trying to be bad, so that they might someday maybe be good; still others are engaged in data-driven arbitrage campaigns so intricate and sophisticated that the actual baseball product seems rather beside the point. This is just how Major League Baseball works at this moment, and while it objectively sucks on its merits, the Angels are at least not one of those teams. They really are trying to win, and over the last five seasons they have mostly lost.

Los Angeles Angels 2021

A club that is run according to a proprietary algorithm or opaque AI protocols or just an overtly cynical financial mandate is at bottom not factoring the interest of its fans into the equation at all. It's a financial gambit, and as such hard to love even when it is also competent enough to be admired. But a team that is run according to the whims of actual humans—one run as a family business, and so uniquely dysfunctional in the ways that only unhappy families can be—can be self-thwarting and repellent in the ways that only humans are. Systems focused on efficiency tend towards degradation; the pressures of the marketplace push the people trapped underneath those rational and merciless structures inexorably down and out. But nothing on earth fucks up quite as consistently or stubbornly as people do. This is what social scientists call "the funny part."

Any family business, if permitted to atrophy over a sufficiently long period of time without any meaningful consequence, will eventually collapse into the dead-star density of the Wilpon-era Mets or the circa-now Trumps—a feudal and floundering enterprise ruled by soggy and unappeasable patriarchs and scrapped over among cruel, lazy, utterly unremarkable heirs from which only certain sour noises can escape. Make *values* the central tenet of an organization and that organization will ultimately be a prisoner of the powerful people whose idiosyncratic ad-hoc values those are. If the owners are sufficiently weird, you wind up with selectively pious and broadly inexplicable organizational philosophies like those seen in Colorado and Kansas City in the last decades. If the owners are just replacement-level rich people, the team will in time come to reflect their bulletproof mediocrity. And if a team is run by a highly leveraged investment group that purchased the team with copious amounts of debt—as the Marlins are, for instance, and as other teams will be as franchise values continue to outrun the prices that even unconscionably rich people can pay—then that team will look and function and feel precisely like what it is, which is a way for investors to claim the annualized return on investment they believe is their right.

Given the realities of that last option, a team and its fans being beholden to one rich man's pride starts to seem comparatively appealing. This has traditionally been a popular model, and not just because the grandiosity of vain rich men has occasionally inspired them to create—or, at least, sufficiently compelled them to allow others to construct—great baseball organizations. But, again, all this is dependent on those men. It's dependent upon the readiness and depth of their wealth, of course, but also and more saliently the scope of their vanity. It is one thing for an owner to view his team as a legacy, a towering accomplishment that he will bequeath to his family and community and The Ages when he's gone; it is another for the owner to consent to let other people, who are not as rich but much more knowledgeable, run the thing.

When and where this works, it works. When it doesn't, you have the Los Angeles Angels of Anaheim, the baseball team owned and controlled by a very rich man named Arte Moreno. In some important ways, the Angels are decently positioned for future success. They have literally the best baseball player on earth and the coolest erstwhile two-way talent in a damn century, a rejuvenated farm system, a hotshot new GM, a new manager with a World Series pedigree, and an owner willing to spend on talent. That all sounds pretty good, and on paper even looks pretty good provided you skim the pitching-related part of the prospectus. But the Angels are still Arte Moreno's team, and so still both very much a family business and an object lesson in being careful what you wish for.

⚾ ⚾ ⚾

"That's not the job it should be," an MLB GM told the *Los Angeles Times'* Bill Shaikin in September, as the Angels prepared to move on from GM Billy Eppler after five years. "It should be a great job. It should be one of the easiest recruitment jobs in the game. Who doesn't want to live there? To me, it's one of the best locations in the world. But something is going on there that is cannibalizing what they're doing."

As a general rule, it is wise to be skeptical about people talking shit anonymously, and doubly so when those people work in baseball. But when Anonymous Shit-Talking GM Guy is right, he's right—if not necessarily about Orange County, which is fine except when and where it's the worst place on earth, then definitely about the tremendous latent potential in the team that plays there. The perception among the MLB execs that spoke to Shaikin was that Moreno's overbearing and overwhelmingly unhelpful ownership was the team's biggest and stickiest problem, and that can be true even if a bunch of anonymous MLB types claim as much. But Moreno's is a very specific type of bad ownership.

The issue is not that Moreno doesn't care about winning, or is unwilling to commit his vast personal fortune to that end; he does, and he has been. The problem is that Moreno wants to win *his way*, with his guys and his hunches and his antique rich guy's conception of what winning baseball is all about. This is something like the single shared value of America's Extremely Rich People; Moreno can see that his team is losing, and hate that, but he is unwilling or unable to adjust any of his curdled priors or loosen his grip even when it has been proven that His Way does not work. If you're rich enough, you can just go on like this indefinitely; baseball, with its clearly delineated and highly public results, tends to make that failure easier to hide.

Moreno has spent the last decade and change sticking defiantly to his guns, nudging and dealing and trying again in the expectation that this time he will turn out to be right. The Angels won the AL West five times during the first six years of Moreno's ownership, although they won just one postseason series during that stretch. Since 2009, the year in which Mike Trout led one of the great June Draft hauls in history, the Angels have made the postseason just once.

Los Angeles Angels 2021

Trout, who has been the best player in the sport since 2012, still has just 12 postseason at-bats. Whatever Moreno is trying to do here has clearly failed, and yet improbably and obstinately it goes on more or less as it has.

Nothing collapsed, exactly, during those years of atrophy and drift. That was the thing: nothing much changed at all. Everything just declined, even as Trout announced himself as the greatest player of his era. To the extent that Eppler succeeded during his tenure as GM, it was in finally forcing some upgrades and updates to an organization that had become expensively and rather proudly dated as it rotely ran it back year after year. Eppler won a power struggle with long-tenured manager Mike Scioscia and replaced him first with Brad Ausmus and then, after just one year, Joe Maddon; Eppler scouted and spent and successfully turned one of the sport's most barren farm systems into one that is if nothing else currently flush in promising outfield prospects. It helped, albeit in ways that are unlikely to benefit the 2021 model.

The team somehow never managed to finish above .500 under Eppler, but the organization that Perry Minasian inherited from him late in 2020 was both more contemporary than it had been and nothing like state-of-the-art. Shaikin noted that the Angels had just 43 baseball operations staffers at the start of the 2020 season, whereas the Dodgers had 62; Moreno furloughed a massive percentage of the club's player development staff and swathes of minor league coaches in June, although the organization brought some cross-checkers back before the draft. In terms of decision-making, no executive has more say than Moreno himself, who obsesses over hiring managers, vetoes his front office's moves when the spirit moves him—he personally shot down a February trade that Eppler worked out with the Dodgers that would have brought in Joc Pederson and Ross Stripling—plays favorites, and is generally always a whim away from reacquiring Vernon Wells. The man's favorite team is the Los Angeles Angels, and he wants them to win the World Series *this year*. The whole organization is pegged to that blank and goofy urge. Of course it doesn't work.

⚾ ⚾ ⚾

Ownership's lack of interest and investment in player development has kept the team stuck in an endless and vexing present in which Trout shines, blameless and brilliant, from the center of a grim maelstrom of imported patches and limping leftovers and readily available non-answers. Every half decade or so, the farm system produces a useful everyday player—David Fletcher really is pretty good, and while Jo Adell was decidedly not in his 2020 debut it would be foolish to stop believing before he's even played in front of fans—and those players slot in wherever there is space. And then it just happens roughly the same way the next year, and the year after that.

It all has managed to remain reliably purgatorial despite Trout's persistent excellence and the tantalizing presence of Shohei Ohtani and Moreno's willingness to buy talent where available. Minasian quickly went to work in the offseason, replacing Andrelton Simmons—there is no greater testament to the void in which this team exists than the fact that it instantly made *Andrelton Simmons* forgettable—with José Iglesias and adding closer Raisel Iglesias and lefty Alex Claudio to the bullpen at a notably minimal cumulative outlay. But it is striking that a team with both Anthony Rendon and Mike Trout still feels so urgently in need of refurbishment. The 2020 season was too short and flukish and grim to mean much, but Adell and Ohtani could hardly have been worse, Justin Upton wasn't much better, and the best pitcher on the roster was either Dylan Bundy or reliever Mike Mayers. That is still true as I write this.

It will surely change, although as always the question is how much. Minasian is not under the same austerity orders as many other big league GM's—Moreno didn't commit to raising the payroll in 2021, but did say "let's put it this way, it's not going down"—and that is an advantage in itself. "One of things that makes this job so intriguing is this is not a 100-loss team," Minasian said in November. "This is not a five-to-seven year rebuild. This is going to be a competitive club." Minasian has displayed a knack in his previous gigs for identifying undervalued talent, but the Angels will need to both pull some gems off the curb and pay MSRP for top-of-the-market talent if they're going to dramatically change their outlook for 2021. This is a heavy lift on its own, but when ESPN's Buster Olney polled former Angels employees in November about how Minasian might make things work in Anaheim, every answer resolved to managing Moreno. It's his team, after all.

Managing Moreno means that longer-term decisions will necessarily take a backseat to near-term ones, which is nothing new. The broader work of building out this organization into something more sustainable, which amounts to making a headstrong and proudly out-of-touch old grouch with a lot of money yield some authority over something he knows nothing about for the first time in his life, is the more difficult bit. That is more or less the challenge facing a great many other American institutions at this moment, as it happens. In sclerotic family businesses as in any other crumbling institution, accountability is the first and most devastating casualty. When the only rule in effect is "the rich guys are going to do whatever they want, without any conceivable consequence" it is not difficult to see how things will unfold, or how they become so difficult to fix.

And yet it would be foolish, here or elsewhere, to say that things can't get better for this team, even if by accident. The Angels have Mike Trout, and Anthony Rendon, and as much Shohei Ohtani as heaven allows, and however much Justin Upton there is left. Even the pitching, which I have politely avoided talking about until this point, has some promise—Dylan Bundy shouldn't be the team's ace, but a rotation that features him and young starters Griffin Canning and Patrick Sandoval could become workable if sufficiently good pitchers are slotted in

Los Angeles Angels 2021

above them all. This is not a division-winning roster at present, but such a team could be built upon it given the necessary resources and room to move. That's a load-bearing "could," but you know that by now.

Given the broader retrenchment in the league and the subsequent shock of this last and mostly lost pandemic season, a sufficiently creative and sufficiently empowered Angels front office *could* flip this gilded dud of a roster into a contender with relative ease. The Angels could be any number of things, up to and including a contender, but what sets them apart, as one of the league's truest family businesses, is that they'll only become what their owner will let them be. They are Arte Moreno's team, no more and no less. They could be something more, but also this is what they are. That's what makes them infuriating, and keeps their circumstances so infuriatingly familiar.

—David Roth is a co-owner at Defector.

Part 2: Player Analysis

Los Angeles Angels 2021

PLAYER COMMENTS WITH GRAPHS

Jo Adell RF
Born: 04/08/99 Age: 22 Bats: R Throws: R
Height: 6'3" Weight: 215 Origin: Round 1, 2017 Draft (#10 overall)

YEAR	TEAM	LVL	AGE	PA	R	2B	3B	HR	RBI	BB	K	SB	CS	AVG/OBP/SLG
2018	BUR	LO-A	19	108	23	7	1	6	29	11	26	4	1	.326/.398/.611
2018	IE	HI-A	19	262	46	19	3	12	42	15	63	9	2	.290/.345/.546
2018	MOB	AA	19	71	14	6	0	2	6	6	22	2	0	.238/.324/.429
2019	IE	HI-A	20	27	4	1	0	2	5	1	10	0	0	.280/.333/.560
2019	MOB	AA	20	182	28	15	0	8	23	19	41	6	0	.308/.390/.553
2019	SL	AAA	20	132	22	11	0	0	8	10	43	1	0	.264/.321/.355
2020	LAA	MLB	21	132	9	4	0	3	7	7	55	0	1	.161/.212/.266
2021 FS	LAA	MLB	22	600	67	23	2	19	68	39	226	5	2	.204/.263/.360
2021 DC	LAA	MLB	22	221	25	8	1	7	25	14	83	1	1	.204/.263/.360

Comparables: Matt Kemp, Jay Bruce, Colby Rasmus

You needn't be a fanatical Annual reader to know of BP's institutional affinity for Adell. He's an easy player to believe in, with his tools and upside evident even before his age allowed him to fully sketch his potential. He did that and more ahead of his debut season, which counterveiled his immense promise as a pithy reminder of the pitfalls of a prospect of his sort. Contact skills often round out later when a prospect has prodigious power, but rarely does a successful major-league hitter carry a 66.5 percent contact rate on pitches in the zone. That was almost 20 percent lower than the 2020 league average, and was also the seventh-lowest single-season rate (minimum 100 PA) since tracking began in 2002. The six players who had a year worse than Adell's 2020 don't inspire confidence outside of Joey Gallo, and the Adam Dunn profile is a perilous path to trod. A sample too small to exempt rookie eligibility provides ample reason to dream on a better second campaign, but this is Anaheim, where Mike Trout goes right and nothing else. As many times as Angels fans were reminded of Trout's 2011 struggles another, more disquieting, name came to mind: Brandon Wood. Adell's DRC+ was actually an order of magnitude worse than Wood's disastrous rookie showing, though there's little reason to expect his career arc to be at all similar. The skillset seems too undeniable, plus the scouting industry misses less than it used to. Considering how his noun-named forebears diverged in their first complete seasons, this comment will likely seem ridiculous or foreboding before long.

YEAR	TEAM	LVL	AGE	PA	DRC+	BABIP	BRR	FRAA	WARP
2018	BUR	LO-A	19	108	160	.391	1.2	CF(16): -0.4, RF(3): -0.9, LF(1): -0.3	0.9
2018	IE	HI-A	19	262	141	.345	2.0	CF(36): -5.6, RF(8): -1.1, LF(7): 0.5	0.7
2018	MOB	AA	19	71	98	.333	-0.3	CF(17): -1.9	-0.1
2019	IE	HI-A	20	27	114	.385	0.3	CF(3): 0.5, RF(2): -0.1, LF(1): -0.1	0.2
2019	MOB	AA	20	182	167	.369	0.5	RF(19): -1.2, CF(17): -3.5, LF(5): 1.9	1.5
2019	SL	AAA	20	132	66	.410	2.5	RF(13): -0.5, LF(9): 0.6, CF(4): -0.7	0.0
2020	LAA	MLB	21	132	46	.258	0.2	RF(34): 0.3, CF(4): 0.5	-0.4
2021 FS	LAA	MLB	22	600	67	.303	0.1	RF 0, CF 0	-0.9
2021 DC	LAA	MLB	22	221	67	.303	0.0	RF 0, CF 0	-0.4

Los Angeles Angels 2021

Jo Adell, continued

Batted Ball Distribution

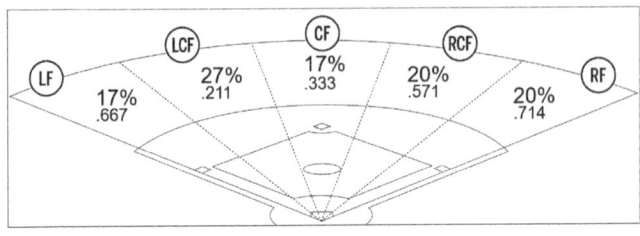

Strike Zone vs LHP

Strike Zone vs RHP

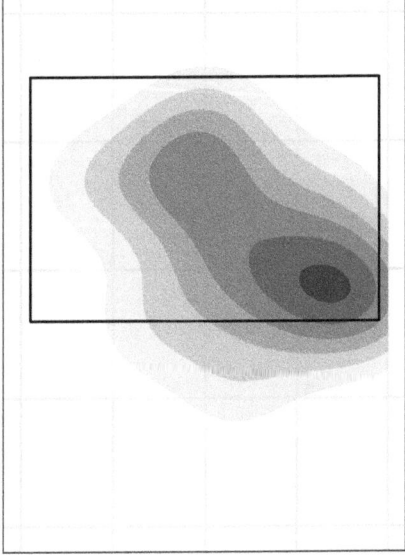

David Fletcher SS

Born: 05/31/94   Age: 27   Bats: R   Throws: R
Height: 5'9"   Weight: 185   Origin: Round 6, 2015 Draft (#195 overall)

YEAR	TEAM	LVL	AGE	PA	R	2B	3B	HR	RBI	BB	K	SB	CS	AVG/OBP/SLG
2018	SL	AAA	24	275	55	25	5	6	37	16	21	7	2	.350/.394/.559
2018	LAA	MLB	24	307	35	18	2	1	25	15	34	3	0	.275/.316/.363
2019	LAA	MLB	25	653	83	30	4	6	49	55	64	8	3	.290/.350/.384
2020	LAA	MLB	26	230	31	13	0	3	18	20	25	2	1	.319/.376/.425
2021 FS	LAA	MLB	27	600	80	30	2	9	54	43	78	6	3	.276/.331/.389
2021 DC	LAA	MLB	27	629	84	31	2	9	56	45	82	7	3	.276/.331/.389

Comparables: Rich McKinney, Chris Sabo, Ray Knight

The David and Goliath comparison is almost too easy—he's listed at a probably generous 5'9", has a contact-oriented, power-averse profile out of line with the modern game, and the man's last name is Fletcher, for god's sake. Fine, a slingshot doesn't quite propel arrows, but still, Fletcher is doing things his own way, and making it work. His .095 isolated slugging is third-worst among batters with at least 1,000 plate appearances since 2018, while his 10.3 percent strikeout rate third-best. The hardest-to-strike out batter in that frame, Andrelton Simmons, recalls the tenuous line walked by the contact-reliant: A little slippage compounds into a lot, and Fletcher is a merely good (rather than all-world) defender, though Simmons' impending free agency might give Fletcher a longer look at short. If double-digit homers aren't coming, the doubles can never dry up without the production doing the same. Still, much like the biblical David, Fletcher is inspiring faith.

YEAR	TEAM	LVL	AGE	PA	DRC+	BABIP	BRR	FRAA	WARP
2018	SL	AAA	24	275	137	.364	3.4	SS(31): 3.4, 2B(18): -1.6, 3B(8): 1.6	2.6
2018	LAA	MLB	24	307	91	.307	3.5	2B(43): 1.8, 3B(33): 4.7, SS(7): -0.6	1.6
2019	LAA	MLB	25	653	100	.317	-4.5	3B(90): 1.5, 2B(42): 1.5, SS(39): -0.5	2.5
2020	LAA	MLB	26	230	105	.348	0.2	SS(27): -0.1, 2B(15): 1.3, 3B(8): -0.3	0.9
2021 FS	LAA	MLB	27	600	99	.307	-0.2	2B 1, SS 0	1.6
2021 DC	LAA	MLB	27	629	99	.307	-0.2	2B 1, SS 0	1.9

Los Angeles Angels 2021

David Fletcher, continued

Batted Ball Distribution

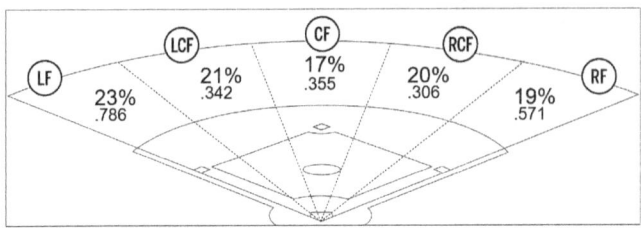

Strike Zone vs LHP

Strike Zone vs RHP

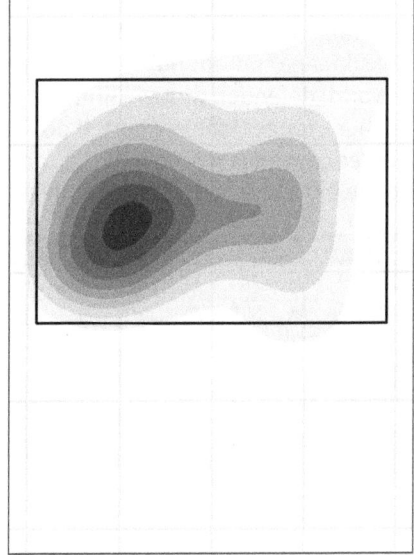

Dexter Fowler RF

Born: 03/22/86 Age: 35 Bats: S Throws: R
Height: 6'5" Weight: 205 Origin: Round 14, 2004 Draft (#410 overall)

YEAR	TEAM	LVL	AGE	PA	R	2B	3B	HR	RBI	BB	K	SB	CS	AVG/OBP/SLG
2018	STL	MLB	32	334	40	10	0	8	31	38	75	5	2	.180/.278/.298
2019	STL	MLB	33	574	69	24	1	19	67	74	141	8	5	.238/.346/.409
2020	STL	MLB	34	101	14	2	0	4	15	10	28	1	1	.233/.317/.389
2021 FS	LAA	MLB	35	600	79	21	2	20	67	75	163	10	5	.223/.332/.394
2021 DC	LAA	MLB	35	326	43	11	1	11	36	41	88	5	3	.223/.332/.394

Comparables: Rick Monday, Mike Cameron, Andy Van Slyke

Fowler built on his solid, if unspectacular, 2019 bounceback by posting a .279/.347/.485 line through August before being sidelined for treatment of his ulcerative colitis. When the lanky outfielder returned three weeks later he cratered, finishing off another replacement-level summer. Fowler's walk and strikeout rates were the worst of his career, he's a double-in-waiting when he stands in right field, and blah blah miserable blah. Let's also not forget his intelligence and openness, his megawatt smile, the way he quietly lives his faith, and his generosity to fans, teammates and needy strangers. There's one season left on Fowler's deal with the Cardinals, during which both sides expected and perhaps deserved a little more from each other. Those five years won't be what he's remembered for.

YEAR	TEAM	LVL	AGE	PA	DRC+	BABIP	BRR	FRAA	WARP
2018	STL	MLB	32	334	77	.210	2.0	RF(75): -4.3	-0.4
2019	STL	MLB	33	574	100	.293	-0.5	RF(118): -0.3, CF(58): -3.4	1.2
2020	STL	MLB	34	101	95	.293	-0.1	RF(27): -2.3	-0.2
2021 FS	LAA	MLB	35	600	100	.285	0.4	RF 0, CF -1	1.2
2021 DC	LAA	MLB	35	326	100	.285	0.2	RF 0, CF -1	0.6

Los Angeles Angels 2021

Dexter Fowler, continued

Batted Ball Distribution

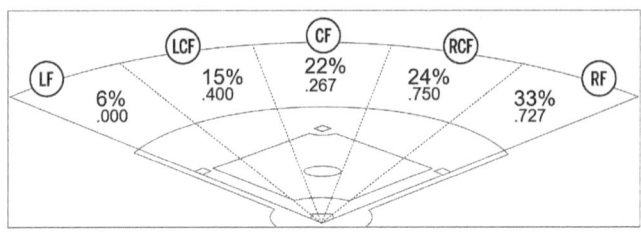

Strike Zone vs LHP

Strike Zone vs RHP

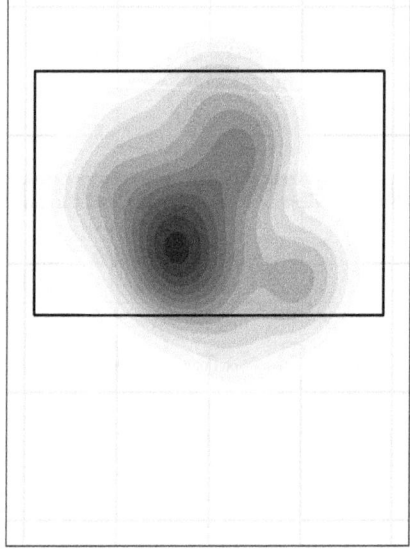

Phil Gosselin 2B

Born: 10/03/88 Age: 32 Bats: R Throws: R
Height: 6'1" Weight: 188 Origin: Round 5, 2010 Draft (#164 overall)

YEAR	TEAM	LVL	AGE	PA	R	2B	3B	HR	RBI	BB	K	SB	CS	AVG/OBP/SLG
2018	GWN	AAA	29	311	38	18	2	5	36	28	59	0	2	.251/.319/.384
2018	CIN	MLB	29	28	5	0	0	1	2	4	8	0	0	.125/.250/.250
2019	LHV	AAA	30	353	54	20	5	8	47	46	61	3	2	.314/.405/.497
2019	PHI	MLB	30	68	5	3	0	0	7	3	16	0	0	.262/.294/.308
2020	PHI	MLB	31	102	14	5	0	3	12	10	27	0	0	.250/.324/.402
2021 FS	LAA	MLB	32	600	56	23	2	13	59	47	151	1	1	.228/.293/.354

Comparables: Gordon Beckham, Iván De Jesús Jr., Matt Kata

"THE GOOSE IS LOOSE," they'd yell in Philly as another Gosselin knock would land on the outfield grass. Largely a spare piece filed away in the minors, the 31-year-old found himself on the big club as he filled the new DH and various infield roles until Rhys Hoskins' injury offered him regular time at first. Gosselin smacked two home runs in his season debut and was hitting .327 with a .944 OPS at the end of August, but fell victim to a September chill with only six hits in 45 plate appearances. "THE GOOSE WAS LOOSE," the people of Philly sadly chanted as his numbers regressed to a far less thrilling slash line and the team drifted out of contention. In another, better season, a player like Gosselin sells T-shirts. In 2020, he supplied another dose of baseball's cruel reality.

YEAR	TEAM	LVL	AGE	PA	DRC+	BABIP	BRR	FRAA	WARP
2018	GWN	AAA	29	311	97	.300	1.0	2B(63): -2.6, 1B(5): -0.7, 3B(4): -0.2	0.1
2018	CIN	MLB	29	28	77	.133	0.3	3B(8): 0.2, 1B(1): -0.0, 2B(1): -0.0	0.0
2019	LHV	AAA	30	353	136	.365	-0.3	2B(58): 1.7, 1B(7): 0.4, 3B(6): 0.1	2.5
2019	PHI	MLB	30	68	74	.347	0.3	LF(6): -0.0, SS(5): -0.5, 3B(1): 0.0	0.0
2020	PHI	MLB	31	102	89	.323	0.7	1B(8): -0.1, LF(7): -0.6, RF(7): -0.5	0.0
2021 FS	LAA	MLB	32	600	78	.290	-0.5	2B 0, 1B 0	-0.2

Los Angeles Angels 2021

Phil Gosselin, continued

Batted Ball Distribution

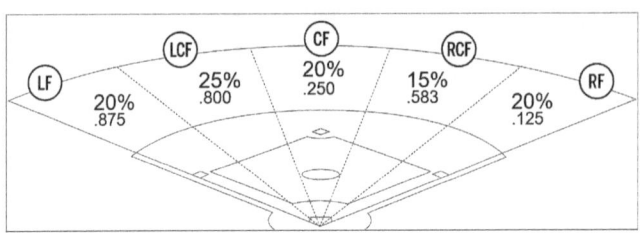

Strike Zone vs LHP   **Strike Zone vs RHP**

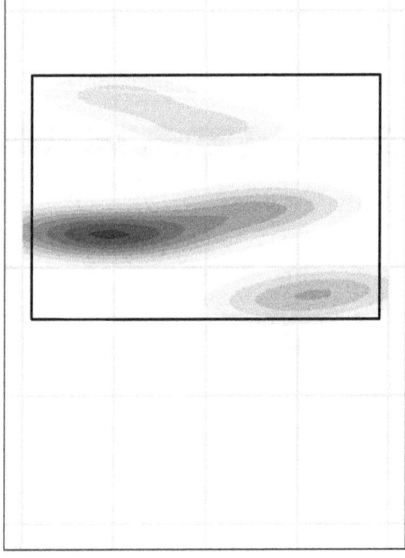

José Iglesias SS
Born: 01/05/90 Age: 31 Bats: R Throws: R
Height: 5'11" Weight: 195 Origin: International Free Agent, 2009

YEAR	TEAM	LVL	AGE	PA	R	2B	3B	HR	RBI	BB	K	SB	CS	AVG/OBP/SLG
2018	DET	MLB	28	464	43	31	3	5	48	19	47	15	6	.269/.310/.389
2019	CIN	MLB	29	530	62	21	3	11	59	20	70	6	6	.288/.318/.407
2020	BAL	MLB	30	150	16	17	0	3	24	3	17	0	0	.373/.400/.556
2021 FS	LAA	MLB	31	600	71	31	1	12	70	28	81	10	6	.263/.308/.390
2021 DC	LAA	MLB	31	564	66	29	1	11	66	26	76	10	5	.263/.308/.390

Comparables: Dale Berra, Kevin Elster, Marco Scutaro

Iglesias on the 2020 Orioles was like a high school senior being forced to play a few games on JV. Despite struggling through multiple leg injuries that limited him to only 22 starts in the field, he had the best offensive year of his career, posting an OPS over .950 and the best expected batting average in baseball. There were moments last year when the O's treated him like a shortstop version of 1988 Kirk Gibson, where Iglesias would enter the game to pinch hit in the late innings, slap a single through the hole and limp his way down to first. It was a weird sight, the slight, slap-hitting shortstop with a career 84 OPS+ before the season, acting like Terrell Owens on one leg in the Super Bowl. Was his sudden sluggage a blip or a breakthrough? That's the Angels' concern now, after they imported Iglesias to backfill a hole left by Andrelton Simmons' free agency. No one can consistently rival Simmons' skill with the leather, but Iglesias should be a solid stand-in, whether he brings his bat or not.

YEAR	TEAM	LVL	AGE	PA	DRC+	BABIP	BRR	FRAA	WARP
2018	DET	MLB	28	464	92	.291	1.6	SS(122): 4.7	2.3
2019	CIN	MLB	29	530	86	.315	3.0	SS(144): 6.5	2.5
2020	BAL	MLB	30	150	111	.407	-0.6	SS(24): -1.4	0.4
2021 FS	LAA	MLB	31	600	90	.289	0.2	SS 2	1.3
2021 DC	LAA	MLB	31	564	90	.289	0.2	SS 2	1.2

Los Angeles Angels 2021

José Iglesias, continued

Batted Ball Distribution

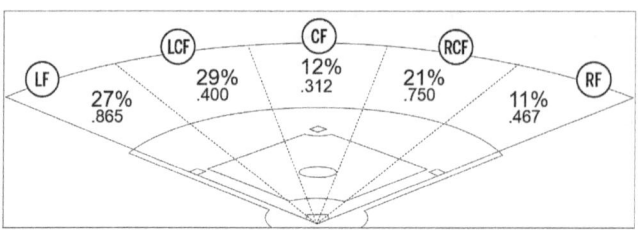

Strike Zone vs LHP   **Strike Zone vs RHP**

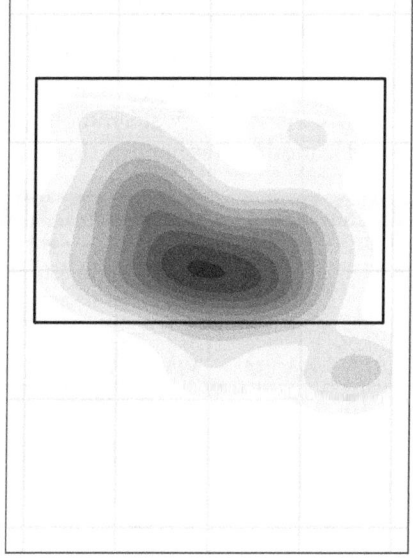

Shohei Ohtani RHP/DH
Born: 07/05/94 Age: 27 Bats: L Throws: R
Height: 6'4" Weight: 210 Origin: International Free Agent, 2017

YEAR	TEAM	LVL	AGE	PA	R	2B	3B	HR	RBI	BB	K	SB	CS	AVG/OBP/SLG
2018	LAA	MLB	23	367	59	21	2	22	61	37	102	10	4	.285/.361/.564
2019	LAA	MLB	24	425	51	20	5	18	62	33	110	12	3	.286/.343/.505
2020	LAA	MLB	25	175	23	6	0	7	24	22	50	7	1	.190/.291/.366
2021 FS	*LAA*	*MLB*	*26*	*600*	*80*	*26*	*3*	*26*	*84*	*60*	*172*	*14*	*5*	*.244/.326/.454*
2021 DC	*LAA*	*MLB*	*26*	*379*	*50*	*16*	*2*	*16*	*53*	*38*	*108*	*8*	*4*	*.244/.326/.454*

Comparables: Craig Wilson, Dave Kingman, Richie Sexson

In Ohtani's first Annual comment three years ago, he was likened to Halley's Comet—a once-in-a-lifetime occurrence people will remember watching for the rest of their lives. That remains true even as it becomes questionable whether the comet has passed us by, leaving us only with the memories. Ohtani's 2020 was a total loss, not only ruining a season but also threatening his viability as a major-league pitcher. Two abortive, disastrous starts featuring sharply diminished velocity—it was even worse than the three mph topline loss, given his 2018 figure was bogged down in his last few starts before shutdown—were all the NPB import got in his third season stateside. Worse than even that, he looked lost, both at the plate and in general. He's running it back for another attempt at a two-way season, but if 2021 goes poorly, it would be unsurprising if we're back to waiting another lifetime for a player of Ohtani's ilk.

YEAR	TEAM	LVL	AGE	PA	DRC+	BABIP	BRR	FRAA	WARP
2018	LAA	MLB	23	367	128	.350	-2.3	P(10): 0.7	1.7
2019	LAA	MLB	24	425	105	.354	-1.5		0.8
2020	LAA	MLB	25	175	87	.229	0.4	P(2): -0.0	0.1
2021 FS	*LAA*	*MLB*	*26*	*600*	*108*	*.310*	*0.9*	*1B 0*	*1.6*
2021 DC	*LAA*	*MLB*	*26*	*379*	*108*	*.310*	*0.6*		*1.1*

Shohei Ohtani, continued

Batted Ball Distribution

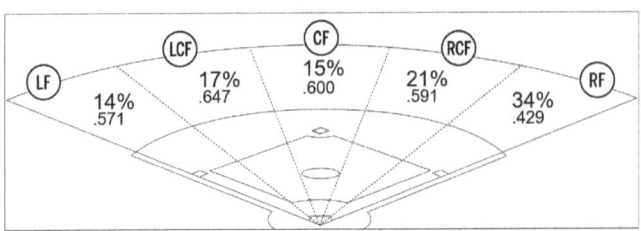

Strike Zone vs LHP   Strike Zone vs RHP

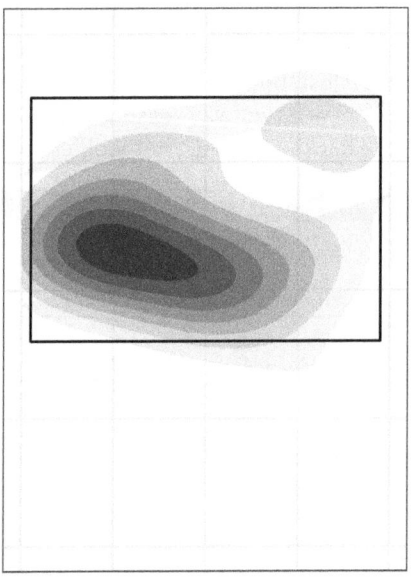

Type	Frequency	Velocity	H Movement	V Movement
● Fastball	48.8%	93.9 [104]	-2.2 [121]	-14.9 [101]
✕ Splitter	16.3%	85.9 [103]	-2.4 [120]	-32 [92]
▽ Slider	28.8%	79.2 [79]	13.2 [130]	-35 [96]
◇ Curveball	6.3%	72 [74]	12 [118]	-60.1 [74]

Albert Pujols 1B

Born: 01/16/80   Age: 41   Bats: R   Throws: R
Height: 6'3"   Weight: 235   Origin: Round 13, 1999 Draft (#402 overall)

YEAR	TEAM	LVL	AGE	PA	R	2B	3B	HR	RBI	BB	K	SB	CS	AVG/OBP/SLG
2018	LAA	MLB	38	498	50	20	0	19	64	28	65	1	0	.245/.289/.411
2019	LAA	MLB	39	545	55	22	0	23	93	43	68	3	0	.244/.305/.430
2020	LAA	MLB	40	163	15	8	0	6	25	9	25	0	0	.224/.270/.395
2021 FS	LAA	MLB	41	600	68	24	0	21	79	39	103	2	1	.236/.290/.395
2021 DC	LAA	MLB	41	442	50	17	0	15	58	28	76	1	1	.236/.290/.395

Comparables: Eddie Murray, Jason Giambi, Rafael Palmeiro

Asked in May whether he planned to return to play past the final season of his ten-year contract in 2021, Pujols demurred that he hadn't "closed that door." Judging by the Coleridge-ian reputation of that contract, you might assume that door had already closed ahead of the 40-year-old, with no window jarring open. It's possible that'll be the case, a decision as much out of his hands as the 312 times he's been intentionally walked (second most all-time). And to say the legendary first baseman wasn't that bad is the loudest damnation, with the faintest of praise. They can't all be Nelson Cruz, loosing the majors' best pure power well into his thirties, and that a 40-year-old who has been in the big leagues for half of his life is still here, almost justifiably, is something. If Pujols can be almost justifiable for 2022, someone will probably justify it. In the meantime, get into the room while you can.

YEAR	TEAM	LVL	AGE	PA	DRC+	BABIP	BRR	FRAA	WARP
2018	LAA	MLB	38	498	101	.247	-1.9	1B(70): 3.8	1.0
2019	LAA	MLB	39	545	98	.238	-5.0	1B(98): -0.4, 3B(1): -0.0	0.2
2020	LAA	MLB	40	163	93	.230	-1.1	1B(26): 2.3	0.1
2021 FS	LAA	MLB	41	600	84	.255	-0.8	1B 0, 3B 0	-0.4
2021 DC	LAA	MLB	41	442	84	.255	-0.6	1B 0	-0.3

Los Angeles Angels 2021

Albert Pujols, continued

Batted Ball Distribution

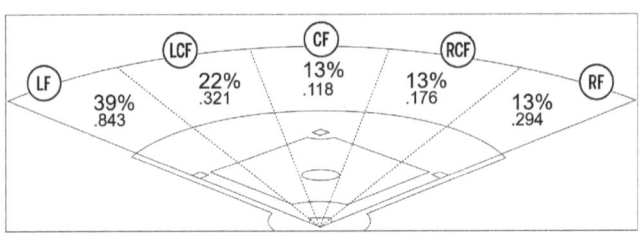

Strike Zone vs LHP   Strike Zone vs RHP

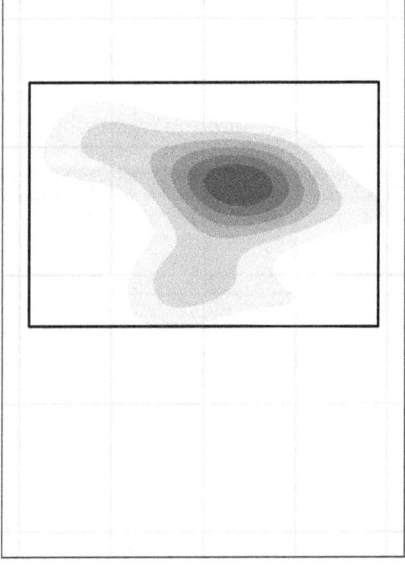

Anthony Rendon   3B
Born: 06/06/90   Age: 31   Bats: R   Throws: R
Height: 6'1"   Weight: 200   Origin: Round 1, 2011 Draft (#6 overall)

YEAR	TEAM	LVL	AGE	PA	R	2B	3B	HR	RBI	BB	K	SB	CS	AVG/OBP/SLG
2018	WAS	MLB	28	597	88	44	2	24	92	55	82	2	1	.308/.374/.535
2019	WAS	MLB	29	646	117	44	3	34	126	80	86	5	1	.319/.412/.598
2020	LAA	MLB	30	232	29	11	1	9	31	38	31	0	0	.286/.418/.497
2021 FS	LAA	MLB	31	600	92	29	1	25	90	78	99	6	3	.271/.378/.486
2021 DC	LAA	MLB	31	639	98	31	1	27	95	83	106	7	3	.271/.378/.486

Comparables: Bill Melton, Howard Johnson, Eric Chavez

If you're looking for reasons to fret, Rendon's never-laudable defense at the hot corner appeared to regress further in 2020, his FRAA the sixth worst in MLB. If you're seizing on that, though, here is some genuine advice for you: Find better things to worry about; there are innumerable contenders. Truly, the former National maintained his forward momentum with the bat from his walk year, hitting nearly as well as the guy who plays center field. Fans can lament the loss of seeing Rendon in person and in pristine form, but there's little reason beyond typical aging concerns to expect a cliff in the next few sixths of his massive contract. And if the defensive slippage portends a shift to first base in the latter half of the six-year deal, well, it's not like the Angels won't have an opening there in the near future.

YEAR	TEAM	LVL	AGE	PA	DRC+	BABIP	BRR	FRAA	WARP
2018	WAS	MLB	28	597	133	.323	2.9	3B(136): -5.7	4.4
2019	WAS	MLB	29	646	150	.323	1.0	3B(146): -4.5, 2B(1): -0.0	6.3
2020	LAA	MLB	30	232	143	.302	0.6	3B(52): -8.4	0.9
2021 FS	LAA	MLB	31	600	136	.292	-0.4	3B -2, 2B 0	3.6
2021 DC	LAA	MLB	31	639	136	.292	-0.4	3B -3	3.9

Los Angeles Angels 2021

Anthony Rendon, continued

Batted Ball Distribution

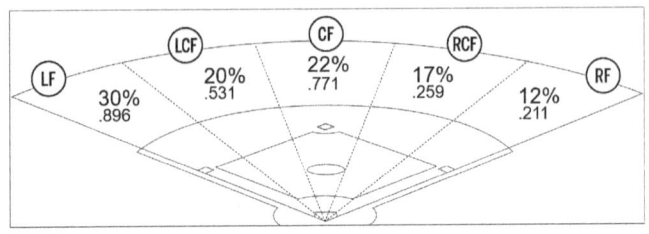

Strike Zone vs LHP   Strike Zone vs RHP

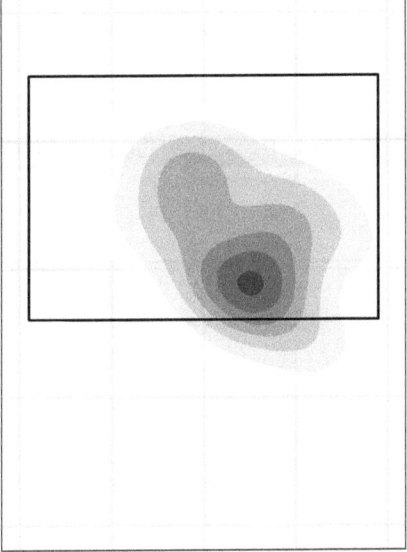

Luis Rengifo 2B

Born: 02/26/97   Age: 24   Bats: S   Throws: R
Height: 5'10"   Weight: 195   Origin: International Free Agent, 2013

YEAR	TEAM	LVL	AGE	PA	R	2B	3B	HR	RBI	BB	K	SB	CS	AVG/OBP/SLG
2018	IE	HI-A	21	190	36	11	3	2	16	27	22	22	8	.323/.426/.466
2018	MOB	AA	21	180	37	10	5	2	21	23	22	13	2	.305/.417/.477
2018	SL	AAA	21	219	36	9	5	3	27	25	31	6	6	.274/.358/.421
2019	SL	AAA	22	122	16	4	1	5	14	11	24	3	3	.273/.336/.464
2019	LAA	MLB	22	406	44	18	3	7	33	40	93	2	5	.238/.321/.364
2020	LAA	MLB	23	106	12	1	0	1	3	14	26	3	1	.156/.269/.200
2021 FS	LAA	MLB	24	600	69	24	3	13	60	60	145	16	9	.222/.307/.355
2021 DC	LAA	MLB	24	126	14	5	0	2	12	12	30	3	2	.222/.307/.355

Comparables: Jurickson Profar, Mark Bellhorn, Tony Bernazard

Despite a career batting line more befitting a catcher, Rengifo impressed in his rookie 2019 with his play at second and surprising pop (18 doubles in just over 400 plate appearances). Playable at short, the overall package was enticing enough the Dodgers made Rengifo the only named Angel in an ultimately scrapped six-player trade that would have returned Joc Pederson, Ross Stripling, and Andy Pages. That would have marked the infielder's third time being traded in as many years, but it's because Rengifo is valued—teams see enticing potential futures, or did, before 2020 dimmed that hope. Without a turnaround next season, expectations will collapse as quickly as the trade that almost moved Rengifo from Los Angeles to Los Angeles.

YEAR	TEAM	LVL	AGE	PA	DRC+	BABIP	BRR	FRAA	WARP
2018	IE	HI-A	21	190	174	.365	2.5	SS(36): 3.9, 2B(2): -0.0	2.3
2018	MOB	AA	21	180	143	.346	-1.0	SS(30): -3.4, 2B(9): -0.8	0.7
2018	SL	AAA	21	219	111	.310	3.3	2B(31): -1.5, SS(16): 0.1	1.0
2019	SL	AAA	22	122	76	.305	-0.4	2B(12): 3.6, SS(12): 0.9, LF(3): 0.5	0.5
2019	LAA	MLB	22	406	84	.300	-0.4	2B(104): -1.6, SS(12): 1.2	0.5
2020	LAA	MLB	23	106	77	.206	1.0	2B(32): -1.0, 3B(1): 0.0, SS(1): -0.0	0.1
2021 FS	LAA	MLB	24	600	86	.280	1.4	2B 0, SS 0	0.8
2021 DC	LAA	MLB	24	126	86	.280	0.3	2B 0, SS 0	0.2

Luis Rengifo, continued

Batted Ball Distribution

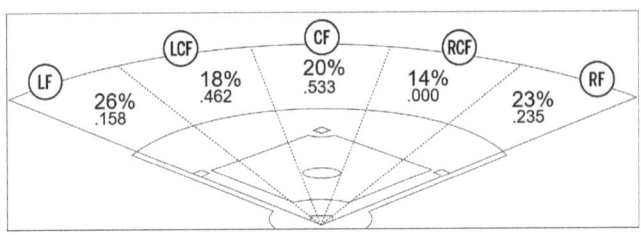

Strike Zone vs LHP **Strike Zone vs RHP**

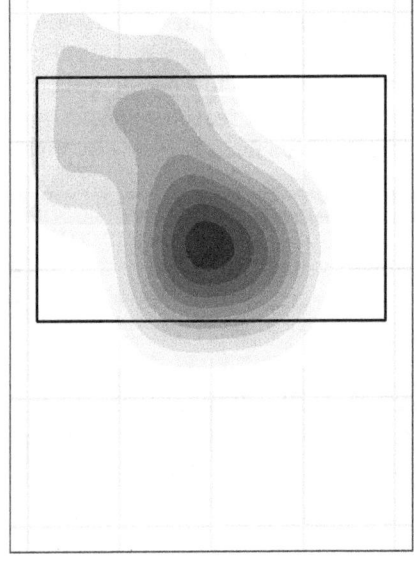

Max Stassi C

Born: 03/15/91   Age: 30   Bats: R   Throws: R
Height: 5'10"   Weight: 200   Origin: Round 4, 2009 Draft (#123 overall)

YEAR	TEAM	LVL	AGE	PA	R	2B	3B	HR	RBI	BB	K	SB	CS	AVG/OBP/SLG
2018	HOU	MLB	27	250	28	13	0	8	27	23	74	0	0	.226/.316/.394
2019	HOU	MLB	28	98	4	1	0	1	3	7	34	0	0	.167/.235/.211
2019	LAA	MLB	28	49	3	0	0	0	2	5	15	0	0	.071/.163/.071
2020	LAA	MLB	29	105	12	2	0	7	20	11	21	0	0	.278/.352/.533
2021 FS	LAA	MLB	30	600	76	24	1	24	75	58	169	0	1	.226/.314/.412
2021 DC	LAA	MLB	30	284	36	11	0	11	35	27	80	0	0	.226/.314/.412

Comparables: Jason LaRue, Tim Laudner, John Russell

YEAR	TEAM	P. COUNT	FRM RUNS	BLK RUNS	THRW RUNS	TOT RUNS
2018	HOU	9684	13.9	0.1	-0.1	14.0
2019	HOU	3717	6.6	-0.2	-0.1	6.3
2019	LAA	2392	3.9	-0.5	-0.1	3.3
2020	LAA	4049	1.5	0.3	0.2	2.1
2021	LAA	10822	7.1	1.6	-0.5	8.2
2021	LAA	10822	7.1	1.3	-0.5	8.0

Sometimes a headline tells you everything you need to know, like "Celebrity Chef's 'Paleo for Babies' Book on Hold Over Infant-Death Fears." In Stassi's case, the headline was "Historically Futile Batter More Than Doubled DRC+ Year-Over-Year." Sure, the prior figure was a 49, but an above-average batting line is a win for any catcher, especially one with Stassi's defensive prowess. There are reasons to expect the breakout at the plate was genuine: He posted marks well beyond career averages in strikeout rate, exit velocity, walk rate, and isolated slugging, plus all the traditional stats. It seems foolish to expect a recurrence, especially once pitchers realize that the jig is up; only six hitters with 100 plate appearances saw more pitches in the zone than Stassi. Not that he's terrible at easing off bad pitches, but more nibbling will require an adjustment. Still, the handling abilities make Stassi a capable backstop even if he regresses to average (for a catcher) at the plate.

YEAR	TEAM	LVL	AGE	PA	DRC+	BABIP	BRR	FRAA	WARP
2018	HOU	MLB	27	250	85	.302	-0.1	C(82): 14.5	2.3
2019	HOU	MLB	28	98	60	.255	-1.3	C(26): 6.1, 1B(3): -0.0, P(1): -0.0	0.5
2019	LAA	MLB	28	49	24	.103	0.0	C(20): 3.4	0.1
2020	LAA	MLB	29	105	117	.277	-0.5	C(31): 0.8	0.9
2021 FS	LAA	MLB	30	600	97	.285	-0.9	C 13, 1B 0	3.6
2021 DC	LAA	MLB	30	284	97	.285	-0.4	C 8	1.9

Los Angeles Angels 2021

Max Stassi, continued

Batted Ball Distribution

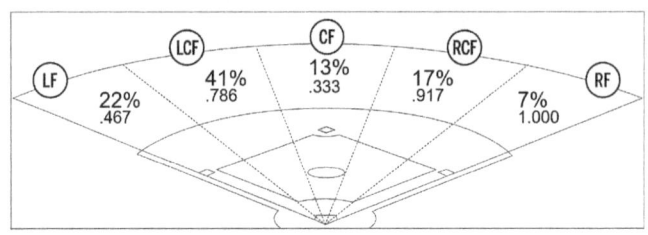

Strike Zone vs LHP   Strike Zone vs RHP

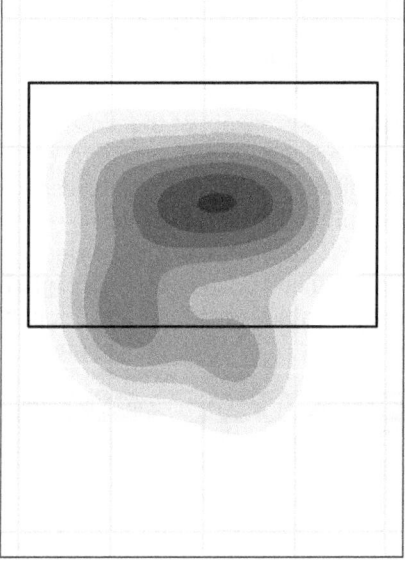

Kurt Suzuki   C

Born: 10/04/83   Age: 37   Bats: R   Throws: R
Height: 5'11"   Weight: 210   Origin: Round 2, 2004 Draft (#67 overall)

YEAR	TEAM	LVL	AGE	PA	R	2B	3B	HR	RBI	BB	K	SB	CS	AVG/OBP/SLG
2018	ATL	MLB	34	388	45	24	0	12	50	22	43	0	0	.271/.332/.444
2019	WAS	MLB	35	309	37	11	0	17	63	20	36	0	1	.264/.324/.486
2020	WAS	MLB	36	129	15	8	0	2	17	11	19	1	0	.270/.349/.396
2021 FS	LAA	MLB	37	600	70	24	0	21	77	37	98	1	1	.244/.312/.410
2021 DC	LAA	MLB	37	296	34	12	0	10	38	18	48	0	0	.244/.312/.410

Comparables: Ramon Hernandez, Yadier Molina, Jamie Burke

Are you in the market for second base? Well, good news—you too can swipe a bag off Suzuki. (Does it matter if you're a catcher, you might ask? No, no, as J.T. Realmuto proved by stealing off Suzuki twice in a single game.) While Suzuki empowers thieves, he himself isn't one, as evidenced by his bottom-scraping framing metrics. He can still hit a little, but given his defensive shortcomings, any team who is willingly playing Suzuki behind the plate is probably losing value.

YEAR	TEAM	P. COUNT	FRM RUNS	BLK RUNS	THRW RUNS	TOT RUNS
2018	ATL	12636	-7.5	1.5	-0.4	-6.4
2019	WAS	10655	-5.9	-1.7	-1.3	-8.9
2020	WAS	4520	-3.6	-0.1	0.1	-3.6
2021	LAA	10822	-7.7	1.1	-0.3	-7.0
2021	LAA	10822	-7.7	1.2	-0.3	-6.9

YEAR	TEAM	LVL	AGE	PA	DRC+	BABIP	BRR	FRAA	WARP
2018	ATL	MLB	34	388	115	.275	-2.0	C(93): -5.5	1.8
2019	WAS	MLB	35	309	115	.248	0.4	C(75): -8.6	1.4
2020	WAS	MLB	36	129	112	.301	-1.5	C(30): -0.7	0.0
2021 FS	LAA	MLB	37	600	96	.263	-1.0	C -10	1.0
2021 DC	LAA	MLB	37	296	96	.263	-0.5	C -7	0.3

Los Angeles Angels 2021

Kurt Suzuki, continued

Batted Ball Distribution

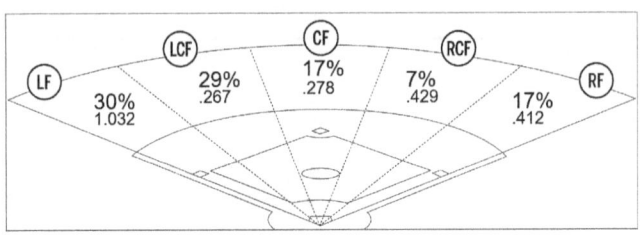

Strike Zone vs LHP   Strike Zone vs RHP

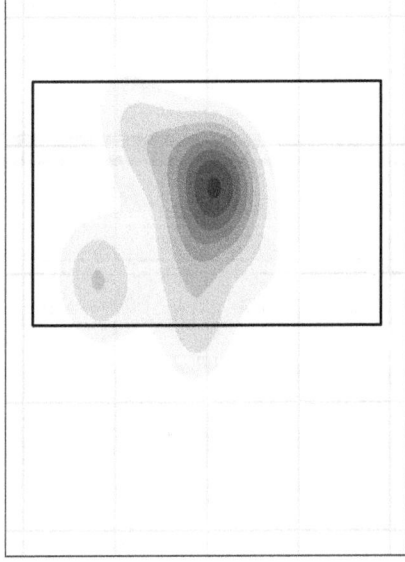

Mike Trout CF

Born: 08/07/91 Age: 29 Bats: R Throws: R
Height: 6'2" Weight: 235 Origin: Round 1, 2009 Draft (#25 overall)

YEAR	TEAM	LVL	AGE	PA	R	2B	3B	HR	RBI	BB	K	SB	CS	AVG/OBP/SLG
2018	LAA	MLB	26	608	101	24	4	39	79	122	124	24	2	.312/.460/.628
2019	LAA	MLB	27	600	110	27	2	45	104	110	120	11	2	.291/.438/.645
2020	LAA	MLB	28	241	41	9	2	17	46	35	56	1	1	.281/.390/.603
2021 FS	LAA	MLB	29	600	112	24	2	36	100	103	141	19	5	.276/.414/.564
2021 DC	LAA	MLB	29	652	122	27	2	39	109	112	153	20	6	.276/.414/.564

Comparables: Mickey Mantle, Eric Davis, Ken Griffey Jr.

Trout is supposed to be a protagonist. Someone of his talents, his evident greatness, has to be bored, uncomfortable with languishing. "How dull it is to pause," and all that. What's a six-year playoff drought but a lacuna, no invitation to the playoff ball a relegation to the sideline. Trout is Ulysses but Trout is Achilles, the most powerful and yet swift-footed, in particular the iteration from Shakespeare's *Troilus and Cressida*. There is no need for introduction, no proof of prowess necessary; he is his own archetype. He is sidelined from the narrative, if not nearly so loudly as *any* Shakespeare character, and though he'd never speak it the team's failure must chafe; Trout can scarce do more to propel the Angels forward but still, "No man is beaten voluntary." Friends with fortune he might be, but soon we will be talking about Trout outrunning time, whether absence from the playoff are enough to make his "deeds forgot." Like all players, Trout's heel is time, and it's well past for the Angels to stop wasting his.

YEAR	TEAM	LVL	AGE	PA	DRC+	BABIP	BRR	FRAA	WARP
2018	LAA	MLB	26	608	183	.346	1.5	CF(125): -2.5	8.2
2019	LAA	MLB	27	600	176	.298	3.4	CF(122): 6.5	8.9
2020	LAA	MLB	28	241	150	.300	0.4	CF(52): -1.8	1.9
2021 FS	LAA	MLB	29	600	164	.317	0.8	CF 0	7.0
2021 DC	LAA	MLB	29	652	164	.317	0.8	CF 0	7.5

Mike Trout, continued

Batted Ball Distribution

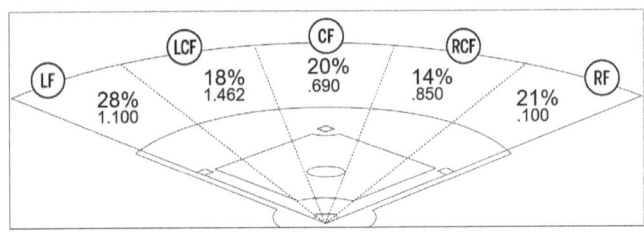

Strike Zone vs LHP

Strike Zone vs RHP

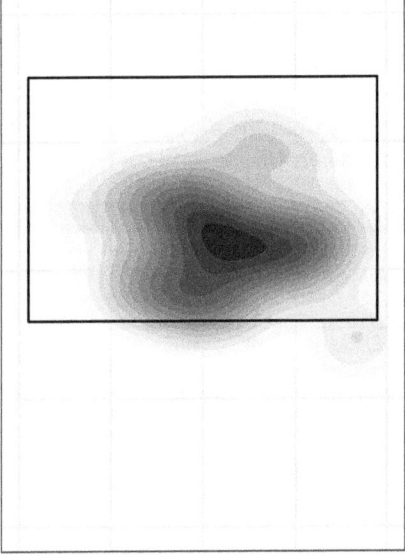

Justin Upton LF

Born: 08/25/87   Age: 33   Bats: R   Throws: R
Height: 6'1"   Weight: 215   Origin: Round 1, 2005 Draft (#1 overall)

YEAR	TEAM	LVL	AGE	PA	R	2B	3B	HR	RBI	BB	K	SB	CS	AVG/OBP/SLG
2018	LAA	MLB	30	613	80	18	1	30	85	64	176	8	2	.257/.344/.463
2019	LAA	MLB	31	256	34	8	0	12	40	32	78	1	1	.215/.309/.416
2020	LAA	MLB	32	166	20	5	0	9	22	11	43	0	2	.204/.289/.422
2021 FS	LAA	MLB	33	600	79	23	0	28	85	60	180	8	4	.231/.319/.439
2021 DC	LAA	MLB	33	537	71	21	0	25	76	54	161	8	3	.231/.319/.439

Comparables: Jonny Gomes, Dan Pasqua, Geoff Jenkins

It's hard to remember, with the perspective of the last two seasons, just how rosy things were looking for Upton after 2018. A season into a five-year extension, he had matched his usual All-Star-level output. The next year brought the most significant injury of Upton's career, a turf toe that cost him the majority of the season and never saw him work up to full strength. A consecutive curtailed season mired in mediocrity makes it hard to see more from the former phenom going forward, though the backloaded final two years of his contract will ensure he'll have numerous opportunities to rebound. The drop in walk rate is a concern, but it doesn't correlate with a major shift in his plate discipline profile, so it doesn't appear as if he's caught Pujolsitis. If you're looking for a reason to get invested in that bounceback, consider that Upton's 1,841 strikeouts already have him 17th all-time; the longer he receives full-time play the better the chances Upton can close the 756 strikeout cushion separating him from Mr. October.

YEAR	TEAM	LVL	AGE	PA	DRC+	BABIP	BRR	FRAA	WARP
2018	LAA	MLB	30	613	116	.321	-1.6	LF(140): 17.0	4.4
2019	LAA	MLB	31	256	91	.261	0.5	LF(56): -3.1	0.1
2020	LAA	MLB	32	166	100	.219	-1.4	LF(39): 0.5	0.2
2021 FS	LAA	MLB	33	600	105	.293	-0.1	LF 4	2.3
2021 DC	LAA	MLB	33	537	105	.293	0.0	LF 3	2.1

Los Angeles Angels 2021

Justin Upton, continued

Batted Ball Distribution

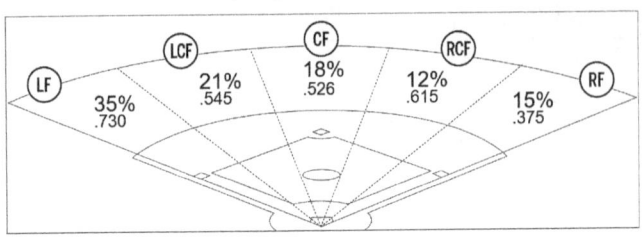

Strike Zone vs LHP   Strike Zone vs RHP

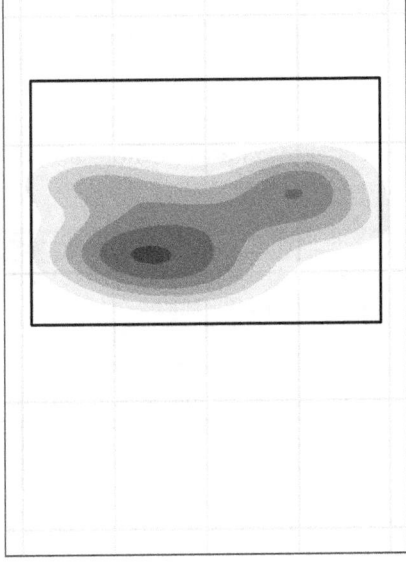

Jared Walsh 1B

Born: 07/30/93 Age: 27 Bats: L Throws: L
Height: 6'0" Weight: 210 Origin: Round 39, 2015 Draft (#1185 overall)

YEAR	TEAM	LVL	AGE	PA	R	2B	3B	HR	RBI	BB	K	SB	CS	AVG/OBP/SLG
2018	IE	HI-A	24	178	28	8	1	13	36	24	50	0	1	.275/.365/.604
2018	MOB	AA	24	173	26	13	0	8	26	21	48	1	0	.289/.382/.537
2018	SL	AAA	24	198	32	13	0	8	37	16	56	0	0	.270/.333/.478
2019	SL	AAA	25	454	90	30	0	36	86	59	115	0	0	.325/.423/.686
2019	LAA	MLB	25	87	6	5	1	1	5	6	35	0	0	.203/.276/.329
2020	LAA	MLB	26	108	19	4	2	9	26	5	15	0	0	.293/.324/.646
2021 FS	LAA	MLB	27	600	85	27	1	29	83	48	157	0	0	.251/.319/.468
2021 DC	LAA	MLB	27	549	78	25	1	26	76	44	143	0	0	.251/.319/.468

Comparables: Mark Hamilton, Rhyne Hughes, Chris Carter

A nominal two-way player, Walsh's more arresting doubling in 2020 was that of his DRC+, raising the possibility that he will be the player to finally unseat Albert Pujols from a starting role. It's unclear whether the Angels still view the otherwise-1B-only slugger, who drew attention by homering six times (and tripling!) in a seven-game stretch in September, as a modern-day Brooks Kieschnick. After being called up at the tail end of August (and totaling 13 plate appearances to that point), Walsh batted 95 times in September, suggesting he'll have plenty of runway next year to continue to prove his offensive worth. Just don't expect a similar breakout pending on the mound—he still barely scrapes 90 with his four-seamer.

YEAR	TEAM	LVL	AGE	PA	DRC+	BABIP	BRR	FRAA	WARP
2018	IE	HI-A	24	178	167	.308	-0.6	1B(26): 0.3, RF(5): 0.7, P(2): -0.0	1.0
2018	MOB	AA	24	173	128	.372	-0.8	1B(37): 2.0, P(2): -0.0	0.5
2018	SL	AAA	24	198	114	.345	1.8	RF(27): -5.7, LF(14): -1.7, 1B(6): -0.2	-0.1
2019	SL	AAA	25	454	145	.374	0.7	1B(58): 4.6, P(13): 0.5, RF(3): -0.0	3.6
2019	LAA	MLB	25	87	58	.349	-0.2	1B(24): 0.6, P(5): -0.0	-0.3
2020	LAA	MLB	26	108	121	.256	0.4	1B(29): -0.9, RF(2): -0.0	0.3
2021 FS	LAA	MLB	27	600	109	.300	-0.9	1B 1, RF 0	1.6
2021 DC	LAA	MLB	27	549	109	.300	-0.8	1B 1, RF 0	1.4

Los Angeles Angels 2021

Jared Walsh, continued

Batted Ball Distribution

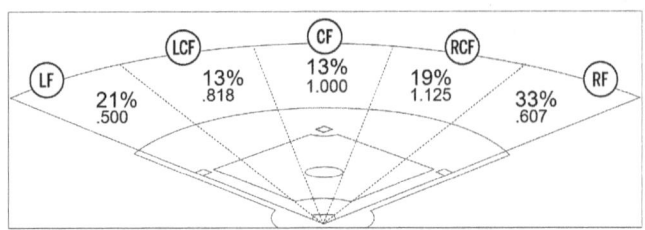

Strike Zone vs LHP   **Strike Zone vs RHP**

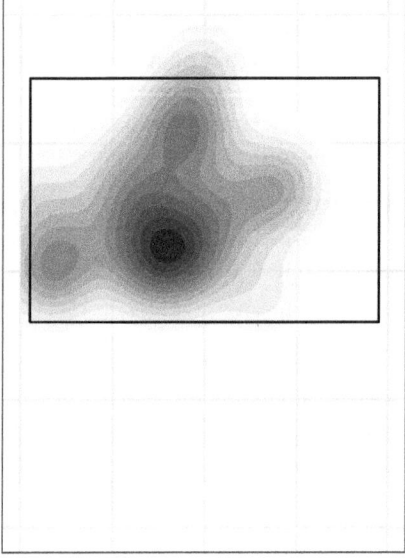

Taylor Ward OF

Born: 12/14/93 Age: 27 Bats: R Throws: R
Height: 6'1" Weight: 200 Origin: Round 1, 2015 Draft (#26 overall)

YEAR	TEAM	LVL	AGE	PA	R	2B	3B	HR	RBI	BB	K	SB	CS	AVG/OBP/SLG
2018	MOB	AA	24	179	26	8	0	6	25	29	33	8	1	.345/.453/.520
2018	SL	AAA	24	267	42	18	0	8	35	36	61	10	2	.352/.442/.537
2018	LAA	MLB	24	147	14	3	0	6	15	9	45	2	0	.178/.245/.333
2019	SL	AAA	25	512	102	34	1	27	71	80	101	11	5	.306/.427/.584
2019	LAA	MLB	25	48	4	3	0	1	2	6	23	0	0	.190/.292/.333
2020	LAA	MLB	26	102	16	6	2	0	5	8	28	2	0	.277/.333/.383
2021 FS	LAA	MLB	27	600	77	25	1	19	72	67	164	1	1	.235/.328/.400
2021 DC	LAA	MLB	27	190	24	8	0	6	22	21	52	0	0	.235/.328/.400

Comparables: Bobby Smith, Russ Davis, Freddy Garcia

Originally drafted as a catcher, Ward saw his bat blossom along with his switch to third base in 2018, and was major-league ready just in time to be blocked by the Angels' signing of Anthony Rendon. A ward without a home, the measure of versatility so many prospects have these days allowed him to nevertheless crack the team's Opening Day roster as a fourth outfielder. While the plate discipline was markedly improved over previous major-league stints, a 27.5 percent strikeout rate is only ever impressive in a relative sense, compared to 2019's mark of 47.9 percent. Without another step, the whispers of a Quad-A profile will linger, especially with Ward having failed to homer in 2020 after 27 in Triple-A the prior season. He should be allowed time at DH next year if nothing else, but as always, our lives balance on the whims of other people.

YEAR	TEAM	LVL	AGE	PA	DRC+	BABIP	BRR	FRAA	WARP
2018	MOB	AA	24	179	186	.409	-1.6	3B(33): -2.8	1.4
2018	SL	AAA	24	267	150	.450	-4.4	3B(53): -10.4	0.6
2018	LAA	MLB	24	147	76	.214	-2.4	3B(40): -2.3	-0.4
2019	SL	AAA	25	512	139	.347	3.0	LF(74): 8.9, 3B(17): -0.6, 1B(6): -0.8	4.6
2019	LAA	MLB	25	48	59	.389	-0.2	LF(9): -0.4, 3B(4): -0.6	-0.2
2020	LAA	MLB	26	102	90	.394	0.8	RF(19): 0.1, LF(17): 0.5, 1B(2): 0.0	0.2
2021 FS	LAA	MLB	27	600	101	.304	-0.9	RF 2, LF 3	1.8
2021 DC	LAA	MLB	27	190	101	.304	-0.3	RF 1, LF 1	0.6

Taylor Ward, continued

Batted Ball Distribution

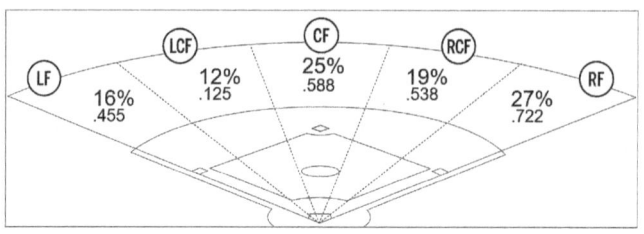

Strike Zone vs LHP   **Strike Zone vs RHP**

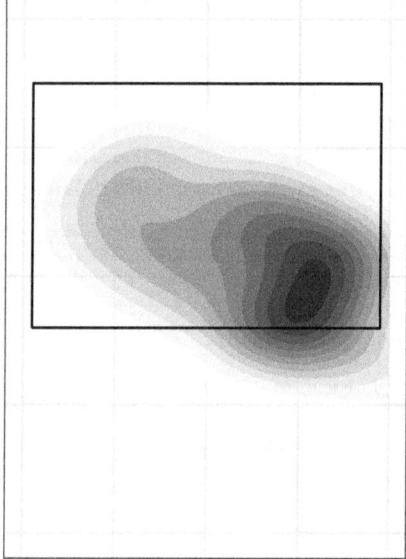

Jaime Barria   RHP
Born: 07/18/96   Age: 24   Bats: R   Throws: R
Height: 6'1"   Weight: 210   Origin: International Free Agent, 2013

YEAR	TEAM	LVL	AGE	W	L	SV	G	GS	IP	H	HR	BB/9	K/9	K	GB%	BABIP
2018	SL	AAA	21	0	0	0	5	5	18	20	2	2.5	9.5	19	28.3%	.353
2018	LAA	MLB	21	10	9	0	27	27	134^1	121	17	3.3	6.8	101	37.0%	.272
2019	SL	AAA	22	3	3	0	10	10	48^1	73	16	1.9	8.2	44	26.3%	.368
2019	LAA	MLB	22	4	10	0	19	13	82^2	92	24	2.9	8.2	75	35.2%	.287
2020	LAA	MLB	23	1	0	0	7	5	32^1	27	3	2.5	7.5	27	33.7%	.261
2021 FS	LAA	MLB	24	9	9	0	26	26	150	146	30	3.2	7.8	129	33.7%	.277
2021 DC	LAA	MLB	24	6	4	0	36	6	76.7	75	15	3.2	7.8	66	33.7%	.277

Comparables: Jordan Lyles, Lucas Giolito, José Berríos

    Barria's 2020 presents a solid argument for those who favor K% to K/9 as an indicator of a pitcher's out-getting prowess. While his K/9 dropped precipitously, Barria's strikeout rate remained level at 20.5 percent; mediocre, but not a reason for concern. If Barria gets to that place in general, it'll be a win after his first two big-league seasons implied he might not be cut out for MLB. His slider is the key; his primary pitch, he managed to avoid throwing it down the middle in 2020, and it showed. The strikeouts per nine vanished simply because Barria wasn't consistently getting into and then working out of jams. He walked fewer batters and allowed fewer baserunners generally, and while we're looking at percentages, he cut his home run rate, season-over-season, a hilarious 65 percent. It amounted to a profile only slightly better than league average, but both pitcher and team will accept that with grace.

YEAR	TEAM	LVL	AGE	WHIP	ERA	DRA-	WARP	MPH	FB%	WHF	CSP
2018	SL	AAA	21	1.39	3.50	98	0.2				
2018	LAA	MLB	21	1.27	3.35	126	-0.5	92.8	49.6%	24.5%	
2019	SL	AAA	22	1.72	9.68	149	-0.3				
2019	LAA	MLB	22	1.44	6.42	158	-1.9	93.2	36.9%	22.2%	
2020	LAA	MLB	23	1.11	3.62	100	0.3	93.8	43.1%	23.1%	
2021 FS	LAA	MLB	24	1.34	4.68	105	1.0	93.2	42.4%	23.2%	47.2%
2021 DC	LAA	MLB	24	1.34	4.68	105	0.4	93.2	42.4%	23.2%	47.2%

Los Angeles Angels 2021

Jaime Barria, continued

Pitch Shape vs LHH	Pitch Shape vs RHH
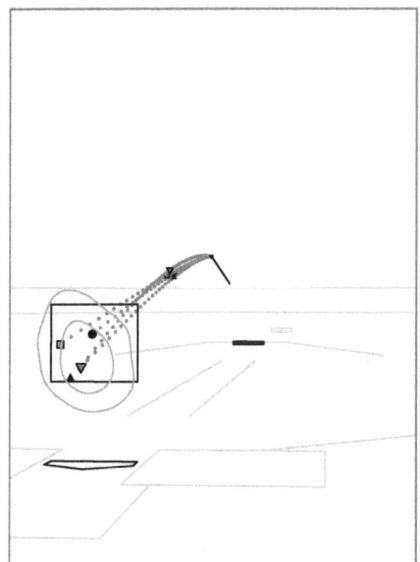	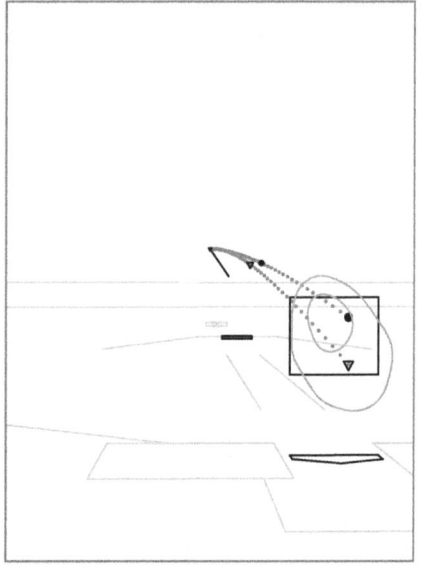

Type	Frequency	Velocity	H Movement	V Movement
● Fastball	31.2%	92.1 [99]	-5.2 [107]	-14.7 [101]
□ Sinker	11.7%	92.1 [99]	-12.8 [102]	-17.1 [111]
▲ Changeup	10.5%	84.1 [96]	-9.1 [114]	-25.4 [106]
▽ Slider	46.0%	84 [100]	3.2 [92]	-30.2 [110]

Dylan Bundy RHP

Born: 11/15/92 Age: 28 Bats: S Throws: R
Height: 6'1" Weight: 225 Origin: Round 1, 2011 Draft (#4 overall)

YEAR	TEAM	LVL	AGE	W	L	SV	G	GS	IP	H	HR	BB/9	K/9	K	GB%	BABIP
2018	BAL	MLB	25	8	16	0	31	31	171^2	188	41	2.8	9.6	184	33.6%	.318
2019	BAL	MLB	26	7	14	0	30	30	161^2	161	29	3.2	9.0	162	41.1%	.297
2020	LAA	MLB	27	6	3	0	11	11	65^2	51	5	2.3	9.9	72	41.0%	.274
2021 FS	LAA	MLB	28	10	7	0	26	26	150	130	23	3.0	9.6	159	39.9%	.279
2021 DC	LAA	MLB	28	11	8	0	29	27	162.3	141	25	3.0	9.6	172	39.9%	.279

Comparables: Jakob Junis, Vince Velasquez, Jon Gray

A new piece of conventional wisdom has taken root in the last few years: If a pitch is bad, the pitcher should stop using it. No, really, that's what has taken teams, pitchers, and the epherma of coaches, trainers, and advisors guiding players more than a century to nail down. Bundy has seen his four-seam fastball velocity dip nearly five ticks since its 2016 peak (not that Bundy was especially effective with heat). So, between 2018 and 2020, Bundy cut his four-seam usage from 48 to 34 percent, remaking himself a junkballer—just one who still strikes batter out. Completing the transformation meant Bundy finally delivered on that fourth-overall pick promise, nearly posting his best season by value in a third of a season. No one can keep ahead of declining velocity forever, unless Bundy is going to be the first pitcher of the 21st century to improve when their fastball velocity dips into the 80s. Which is not to say it's impossible; the man already survived the Orioles pitching development system.

YEAR	TEAM	LVL	AGE	WHIP	ERA	DRA-	WARP	MPH	FB%	WHF	CSP
2018	BAL	MLB	25	1.41	5.45	119	-0.1	93.5	55.8%	26.9%	
2019	BAL	MLB	26	1.35	4.79	100	1.6	93.0	50.0%	28.2%	
2020	LAA	MLB	27	1.04	3.29	78	1.4	92.2	41.9%	29.5%	
2021 FS	LAA	MLB	28	1.21	3.63	85	2.7	92.9	49.3%	28.2%	48.5%
2021 DC	LAA	MLB	28	1.21	3.63	85	2.9	92.9	49.3%	28.2%	48.5%

Los Angeles Angels 2021

Dylan Bundy, continued

Pitch Shape vs LHH

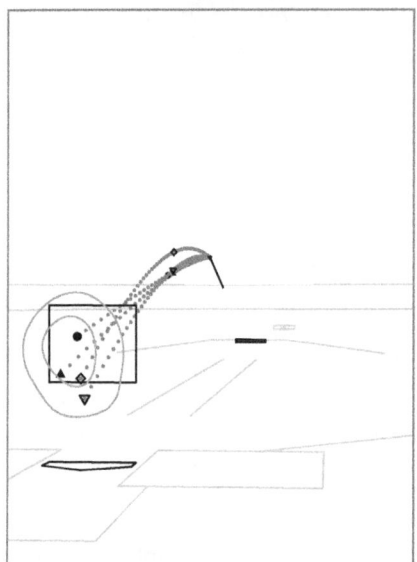

Pitch Shape vs RHH

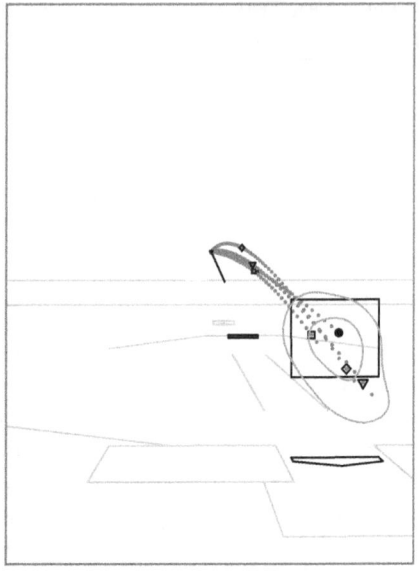

Type	Frequency	Velocity	H Movement	V Movement
● Fastball	33.5%	90.1 [92]	-4.3 [111]	-13.3 [105]
□ Sinker	8.3%	90.7 [91]	-11.4 [112]	-15.6 [116]
▲ Changeup	21.3%	82.3 [89]	-11.5 [101]	-28.6 [97]
▽ Slider	25.0%	80 [82]	3.9 [95]	-39.1 [85]
◇ Curveball	11.7%	73.5 [80]	7.3 [99]	-57.3 [80]

Ty Buttrey   RHP

Born: 03/31/93   Age: 28   Bats: L   Throws: R
Height: 6'6"   Weight: 240   Origin: Round 4, 2012 Draft (#151 overall)

YEAR	TEAM	LVL	AGE	W	L	SV	G	GS	IP	H	HR	BB/9	K/9	K	GB%	BABIP
2018	WOR	AAA	25	1	1	1	32	0	44	36	4	2.9	13.1	64	45.2%	.320
2018	LAA	MLB	25	0	1	4	16	0	16^1	15	0	2.8	11.0	20	55.6%	.341
2019	LAA	MLB	26	6	7	2	72	0	72^1	69	8	2.9	10.5	84	44.7%	.323
2020	LAA	MLB	27	2	3	5	27	0	26^1	28	4	3.1	6.2	18	47.6%	.304
2021 FS	LAA	MLB	28	2	2	4	57	0	50	45	6	3.8	9.3	51	45.8%	.292
2021 DC	LAA	MLB	28	2	2	4	57	0	51.3	46	6	3.8	9.3	52	45.8%	.292

Comparables: Jordan Walden, Dovydas Neverauskas, Michael Feliz

By the 2019 All-Star Break, Buttrey seemed to have cemented himself in the Angels' bullpen: Through his first 58 1/3 career innings, he posted a 2.78 ERA with 70 strikeouts. In 56 2/3 innings since, with a 5.78 ERA and 52 punchouts, Buttrey has torched his reputation worse than the final episode of *Dexter*. The reliever's malady is hard to diagnose; you don't double your ERA going from 98-and-a-slider to 97-and-a-slider. His fastball lost some of its drop, and hitters squared up on it, driving up his contact rate nearly 10 percent across the board. It wouldn't be the first time something got predictable in later seasons. Like Showtime's first hit show, though, the promise of a legitimate star reliever will keep the Angels trusting Buttrey as long as they can justify, maybe beyond. Some allusion to a return to form, though, will swiftly become necessary if the Angels ever start needing relievers for games that matter. No one wants to be remembered only for an irredeemable finale.

YEAR	TEAM	LVL	AGE	WHIP	ERA	DRA-	WARP	MPH	FB%	WHF	CSP
2018	WOR	AAA	25	1.14	2.25	58	1.1				
2018	LAA	MLB	25	1.22	3.31	64	0.4	98.3	58.0%	30.1%	
2019	LAA	MLB	26	1.27	3.98	72	1.4	98.8	57.2%	27.2%	
2020	LAA	MLB	27	1.41	5.81	102	0.2	97.9	58.2%	20.0%	
2021 FS	LAA	MLB	28	1.33	4.05	92	0.5	98.5	57.5%	25.1%	48.3%
2021 DC	LAA	MLB	28	1.33	4.05	92	0.5	98.5	57.5%	25.1%	48.3%

Los Angeles Angels 2021

Ty Buttrey, continued

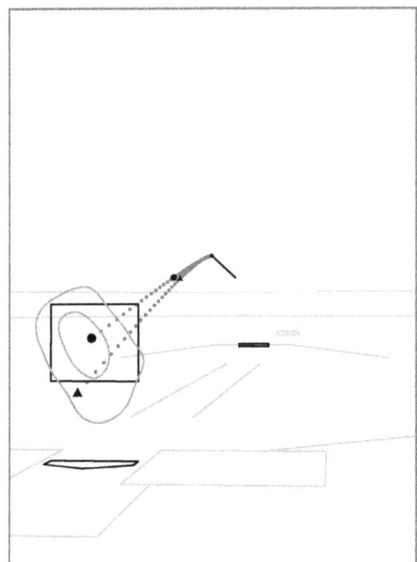
Pitch Shape vs LHH

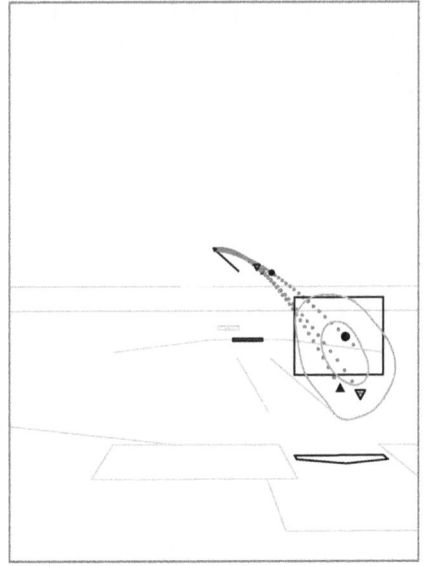
Pitch Shape vs RHH

Type	Frequency	Velocity	H Movement	V Movement
● Fastball	56.8%	96.2 [111]	-11.9 [75]	-14.8 [101]
▲ Changeup	19.2%	86.3 [104]	-15.2 [82]	-30.4 [92]
▽ Slider	21.7%	82.3 [93]	0.6 [83]	-38.3 [87]

Griffin Canning   RHP

Born: 05/11/96   Age: 25   Bats: R   Throws: R
Height: 6'2"   Weight: 180   Origin: Round 2, 2017 Draft (#47 overall)

YEAR	TEAM	LVL	AGE	W	L	SV	G	GS	IP	H	HR	BB/9	K/9	K	GB%	BABIP
2018	IE	HI-A	22	0	0	0	2	2	8^2	4	0	3.1	12.5	12	50.0%	.222
2018	MOB	AA	22	1	0	0	10	10	45^2	27	2	3.7	9.7	49	45.9%	.229
2018	SL	AAA	22	3	3	0	13	13	59	68	6	3.4	9.8	64	40.9%	.378
2019	SL	AAA	23	1	0	0	3	3	16	13	0	1.1	9.6	17	39.0%	.317
2019	LAA	MLB	23	5	6	0	18	17	90^1	80	14	3.0	9.6	96	36.8%	.281
2020	LAA	MLB	24	2	3	0	11	11	56^1	54	8	3.7	8.9	56	36.1%	.307
2021 FS	LAA	MLB	25	9	8	0	26	26	150	136	24	3.9	9.3	155	37.8%	.285
2021 DC	LAA	MLB	25	8	7	0	25	24	123.7	113	20	3.9	9.3	128	37.8%	.285

Comparables: Zac Gallen, Mitch Keller, Zack Wheeler

Canning can't claim canny command, can't uncan 98 mph heaters like seemingly most of the league these days, saw his UCL cankered by damage that ultimately didn't derail his canter of a season. He probably won't be canonized into the brief set of Angels aces anytime soon, instead settling in his second season into more of an average, end-rotation arm. He caught enough can-of-corns to win his first Gold Glove, at least. Canvassing for a pitcher to use their fastball less isn't exactly revolutionary these days, but Canning has a decent cantrip in his curveball and could stand to cannibalize his fastball usage further. Canceling the Tommy John surgery might mean this year's step back is the new normal, but candidly, the Angels would be perfectly canty with their farm system producing any reliable starter.

YEAR	TEAM	LVL	AGE	WHIP	ERA	DRA-	WARP	MPH	FB%	WHF	CSP
2018	IE	HI-A	22	0.81	0.00	16	0.5				
2018	MOB	AA	22	1.01	1.97	81	0.8				
2018	SL	AAA	22	1.53	5.49	83	1.1				
2019	SL	AAA	23	0.94	0.56	42	0.7				
2019	LAA	MLB	23	1.22	4.58	92	1.2	95.5	42.1%	32.3%	
2020	LAA	MLB	24	1.37	3.99	102	0.4	94.2	40.5%	27.3%	
2021 FS	LAA	MLB	25	1.35	4.34	98	1.6	94.9	41.3%	29.9%	44.0%
2021 DC	LAA	MLB	25	1.35	4.34	98	1.4	94.9	41.3%	29.9%	44.0%

Los Angeles Angels 2021

Griffin Canning, continued

Pitch Shape vs LHH

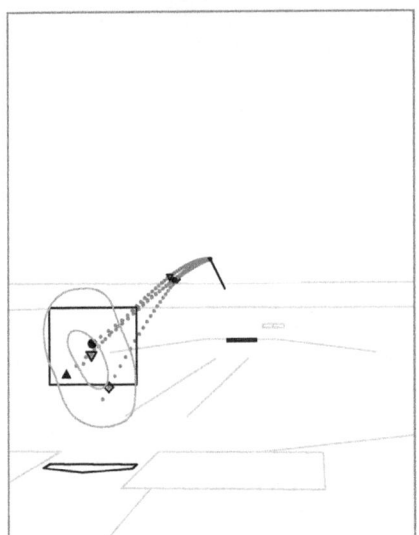

Pitch Shape vs RHH

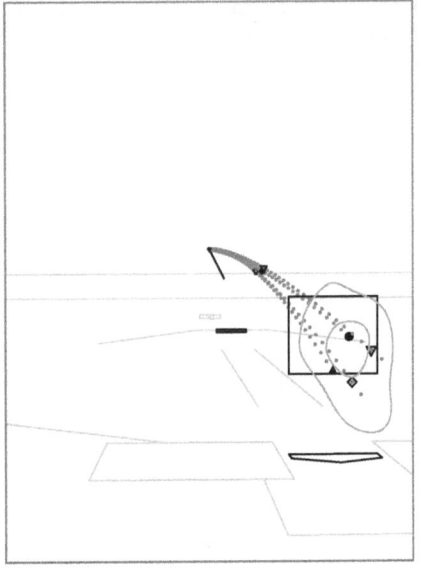

Type	Frequency	Velocity	H Movement	V Movement
● Fastball	40.5%	92.8 [101]	-7.6 [96]	-12.4 [108]
▲ Changeup	15.4%	88 [111]	-13.3 [91]	-23.8 [110]
▽ Slider	19.9%	88.7 [121]	0.5 [82]	-23.8 [129]
◇ Curveball	23.0%	86.6 [131]	-0.5 [67]	-34.6 [131]

Alex Claudio LHP

Born: 01/31/92   Age: 29   Bats: L   Throws: L
Height: 6'3"   Weight: 188   Origin: Round 27, 2010 Draft (#826 overall)

YEAR	TEAM	LVL	AGE	W	L	SV	G	GS	IP	H	HR	BB/9	K/9	K	GB%	BABIP
2018	TEX	MLB	26	4	2	1	66	1	68^1	91	4	1.7	5.4	41	62.0%	.370
2019	MIL	MLB	27	2	2	0	83	0	62	57	8	3.5	6.4	44	56.0%	.268
2020	MIL	MLB	28	0	0	1	20	0	19	18	2	2.8	7.1	15	45.8%	.281
2021 FS	*LAA*	*MLB*	*29*	*2*	*2*	*0*	*57*	*0*	*50*	*49*	*6*	*2.5*	*7.1*	*39*	*54.7%*	*.289*
2021 DC	*LAA*	*MLB*	*29*	*2*	*2*	*0*	*57*	*0*	*40*	*39*	*4*	*2.5*	*7.1*	*31*	*54.7%*	*.289*

Comparables: Cam Bedrosian, Dominic Leone, Michael Lorenzen

Alex Claudio wouldn't have gotten this far if he couldn't surprisingly invent stuff that works from time to time, but it's hard to see how he survives for long in a three-batter-minimum league.

YEAR	TEAM	LVL	AGE	WHIP	ERA	DRA-	WARP	MPH	FB%	WHF	CSP
2018	TEX	MLB	26	1.52	4.48	104	0.2	87.6	52.0%	24.7%	
2019	MIL	MLB	27	1.31	4.06	101	0.3	87.4	46.2%	24.7%	
2020	MIL	MLB	28	1.26	4.26	98	0.2	87.2	39.3%	26.0%	
2021 FS	*LAA*	*MLB*	*29*	*1.27*	*3.80*	*89*	*0.5*	*87.4*	*46.0%*	*25.0%*	*42.3%*
2021 DC	*LAA*	*MLB*	*29*	*1.27*	*3.80*	*89*	*0.4*	*87.4*	*46.0%*	*25.0%*	*42.3%*

Los Angeles Angels 2021

Alex Claudio, continued

Pitch Shape vs LHH

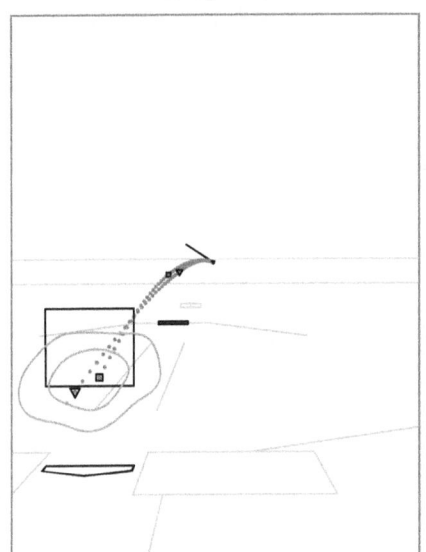

Pitch Shape vs RHH

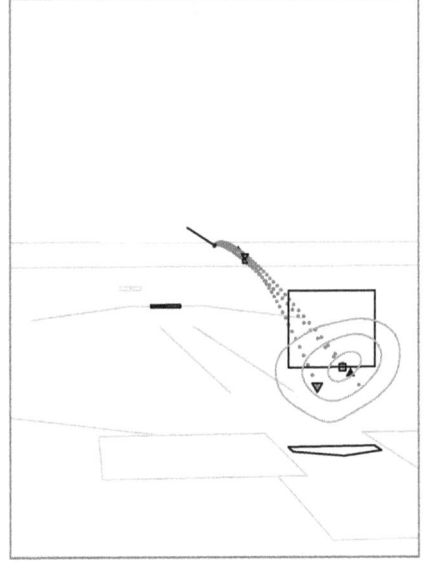

Type	Frequency	Velocity	H Movement	V Movement
☐ Sinker	39.3%	86.1 [67]	15 [86]	-35.2 [53]
▲ Changeup	38.1%	73 [53]	17.1 [71]	-46.2 [49]
▽ Slider	22.7%	76.6 [67]	-5.9 [102]	-40.8 [80]

Alex Cobb RHP

Born: 10/07/87   Age: 33   Bats: R   Throws: R
Height: 6'3"   Weight: 205   Origin: Round 4, 2006 Draft (#109 overall)

YEAR	TEAM	LVL	AGE	W	L	SV	G	GS	IP	H	HR	BB/9	K/9	K	GB%	BABIP
2018	BAL	MLB	30	5	15	0	28	28	152^1	172	24	2.5	6.0	102	49.6%	.305
2019	BAL	MLB	31	0	2	0	3	3	12^1	21	9	1.5	5.8	8	48.0%	.293
2020	BAL	MLB	32	2	5	0	10	10	52^1	52	8	3.1	6.5	38	54.2%	.275
2021 FS	*LAA*	*MLB*	*33*	*9*	*9*	*0*	*26*	*26*	*150*	*156*	*25*	*3.0*	*6.7*	*111*	*50.5%*	*.288*
2021 DC	*LAA*	*MLB*	*33*	*8*	*8*	*0*	*29*	*25*	*137.3*	*143*	*23*	*3.0*	*6.7*	*101*	*50.5%*	*.288*

Comparables: Jeremy Hellickson, Jhoulys Chacín, Matt Garza

Didn't watch a Cobb start this year? That's alright, gather round and we'll fill you in. There were two really good ones, a bunch of average ones and some real Pepé Le Pews. That's life as Alex Cobb, who, when healthy, is about as average a starting pitcher as you'll find. But coming off a three-start, injury-plagued 2019, his impressively forgettable 2020 was actually quite the delight. A man who once upon a time (back in 2013) started and won a Wild Card game for Tampa, Cobb is a different animal now. Tommy John surgery stole his split-change, and Father Time stole his durability. Set to become a free agent after the 2021 season, Cobb floats in this weird, nebulous void of Oriole-dom. He is not a part of Baltimore's future, nor was he a part of its past. He is invisible in plain sight. He's who pitches on nights you don't turn on MASN because you have errands to run, friends to see, a life to lead. And so goes Cobb, who will keep right on pitching, whether you notice him or not.

YEAR	TEAM	LVL	AGE	WHIP	ERA	DRA-	WARP	MPH	FB%	WHF	CSP
2018	BAL	MLB	30	1.41	4.90	122	-0.3	93.3	51.5%	17.7%	
2019	BAL	MLB	31	1.86	10.95	169	-0.3	93.3	47.8%	24.3%	
2020	BAL	MLB	32	1.34	4.30	100	0.5	93.7	48.1%	23.6%	
2021 FS	*LAA*	*MLB*	*33*	*1.38*	*4.65*	*106*	*0.9*	*93.5*	*49.6%*	*20.9%*	*47.4%*
2021 DC	*LAA*	*MLB*	*33*	*1.38*	*4.65*	*106*	*0.8*	*93.5*	*49.6%*	*20.9%*	*47.4%*

Los Angeles Angels 2021

Alex Cobb, continued

Pitch Shape vs LHH
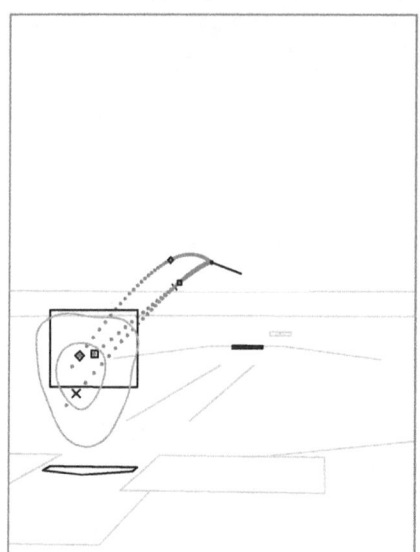

Pitch Shape vs RHH
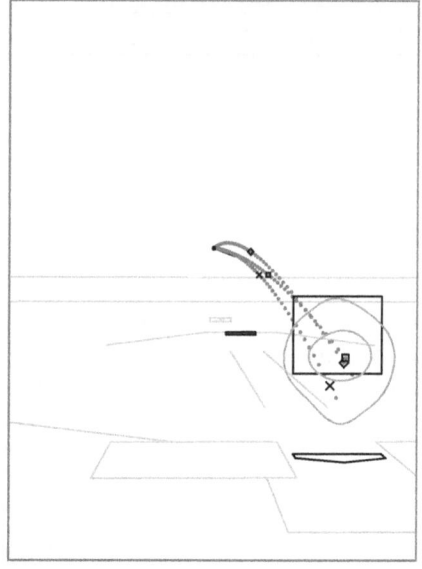

Type	Frequency	Velocity	H Movement	V Movement
☐ Sinker	47.5%	92.6 [101]	-13.2 [99]	-17.1 [111]
✕ Splitter	35.2%	87 [108]	-11.3 [87]	-28.9 [102]
◇ Curveball	16.7%	81.8 [112]	3.5 [83]	-47.9 [101]

Junior Guerra RHP

Born: 01/16/85   Age: 36   Bats: R   Throws: R
Height: 6'0"   Weight: 235   Origin: International Free Agent, 2001

YEAR	TEAM	LVL	AGE	W	L	SV	G	GS	IP	H	HR	BB/9	K/9	K	GB%	BABIP
2018	MIL	MLB	33	7	9	0	32	27	147	151	21	3.4	8.7	142	42.7%	.318
2019	MIL	MLB	34	9	5	3	72	0	83^2	58	11	3.9	8.3	77	43.2%	.221
2020	ARI	MLB	35	1	2	0	25	0	23^2	17	1	5.7	8.0	21	46.2%	.258
2021 FS	LAA	MLB	36	2	2	0	57	0	50	46	6	4.4	8.1	45	44.7%	.282

Comparables: Ian Kennedy, Jeff Samardzija, Mike Fiers

If you like wine and you don't like paying a ton for it, it's likely you spend an inordinate amount of time browsing the aisles at Trader Joe's. The selection is massive and every label showcases tasting notes that don't seem to match the price point. Blackberry, overripe plum, vanilla and tobacco for just six bucks? What a steal! Then, upon consumption, yeah, this tastes like a $6 bottle of wine. For 10 times as much money you could score something actually remarkable. Considering that dinner tonight consists of Trader Joe's lasagna, however, a $6 wine may actually be the right call. There's something to be said for a proper pairing, after all.

YEAR	TEAM	LVL	AGE	WHIP	ERA	DRA-	WARP	MPH	FB%	WHF	CSP
2018	MIL	MLB	33	1.41	4.16	100	1.3	95.1	69.0%	24.8%	
2019	MIL	MLB	34	1.12	3.55	82	1.2	96.1	60.2%	25.9%	
2020	ARI	MLB	35	1.35	3.04	96	0.3	95.3	60.6%	26.9%	
2021 FS	LAA	MLB	36	1.41	4.28	101	0.2	95.6	63.6%	25.7%	45.5%

Los Angeles Angels 2021

Junior Guerra, continued

Pitch Shape vs LHH	Pitch Shape vs RHH
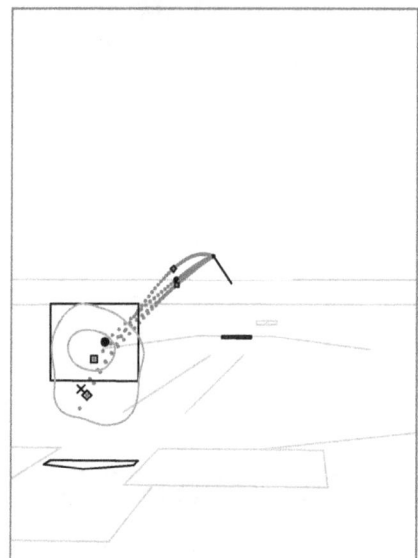	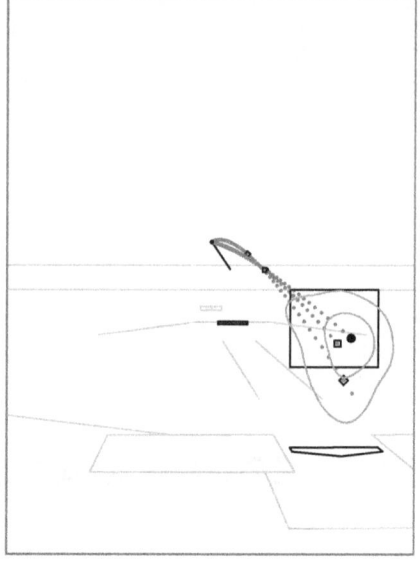

Type	Frequency	Velocity	H Movement	V Movement
● Fastball	33.3%	93.9 [104]	-4.5 [110]	-11.3 [111]
☐ Sinker	26.2%	94.1 [108]	-11 [115]	-13.5 [123]
✕ Splitter	17.2%	86 [104]	-7.6 [101]	-21.2 [127]
◇ Curveball	21.1%	81.7 [112]	5 [89]	-45.2 [107]

Andrew Heaney LHP

Born: 06/05/91 Age: 30 Bats: L Throws: L
Height: 6'2" Weight: 200 Origin: Round 1, 2012 Draft (#9 overall)

YEAR	TEAM	LVL	AGE	W	L	SV	G	GS	IP	H	HR	BB/9	K/9	K	GB%	BABIP
2018	IE	HI-A	27	1	0	0	1	1	6^1	2	0	1.4	8.5	6	73.3%	.133
2018	LAA	MLB	27	9	10	0	31	31	185	179	29	2.2	9.0	184	41.9%	.299
2019	LAA	MLB	28	4	6	0	18	18	95^1	93	20	2.8	11.1	118	32.7%	.312
2020	LAA	MLB	29	4	3	0	12	12	66^2	63	9	2.6	9.4	70	38.3%	.302
2021 FS	LAA	MLB	30	9	8	0	26	26	150	138	27	2.7	10.0	167	37.8%	.293
2021 DC	LAA	MLB	30	9	7	0	25	25	145	134	26	2.7	10.0	161	37.8%	.293

Comparables: Nick Tropeano, Kevin Gausman, Alex Wood

Heaney has a career like a sine wave: He's always up and down, never stretching the amplitude quite so far. He reached an upper bound not so far back, and if down was the only way to go from there, it's not his fault. It's just how the equation, written into the DNA of his arm, was written. His velocity waned, even as his groundball rate pulled out of its own nadir; his contact rate spiked, even while he got ahead in the count at new levels of success. It might not add up to the most interesting problem, but then math has always bored some. Still, coming up on his walk year, Heaney continues to intrigue for the same reason math's ability to predict intoxicates: If you know the function, you can predict where the curve is going next. Crucially, though, you have to get the math right, because Heaney's next step, free agency, will check your work.

YEAR	TEAM	LVL	AGE	WHIP	ERA	DRA-	WARP	MPH	FB%	WHF	CSP
2018	IE	HI-A	27	0.47	1.42	70	0.1				
2018	LAA	MLB	27	1.22	4.14	81	3.5	94.3	58.1%	26.5%	
2019	LAA	MLB	28	1.29	4.91	108	0.5	94.3	58.0%	31.3%	
2020	LAA	MLB	29	1.23	4.46	89	1.0	93.4	58.0%	28.0%	
2021 FS	LAA	MLB	30	1.23	3.98	92	2.1	94.0	58.0%	28.7%	50.4%
2021 DC	LAA	MLB	30	1.23	3.98	92	2.1	94.0	58.0%	28.7%	50.4%

Los Angeles Angels 2021

Andrew Heaney, continued

Pitch Shape vs LHH

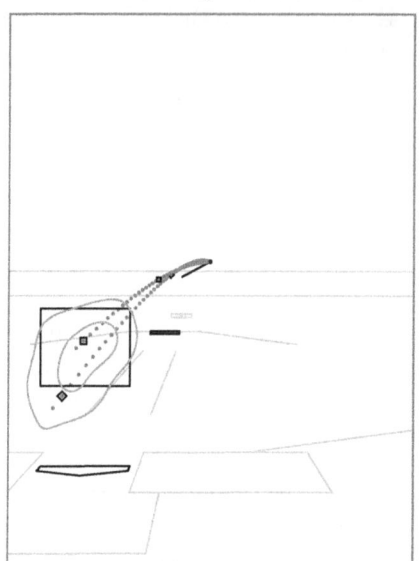

Pitch Shape vs RHH

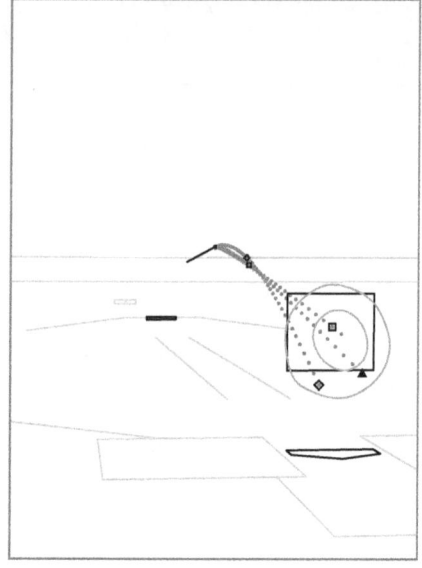

Type	Frequency	Velocity	H Movement	V Movement
☐ Sinker	57.8%	91.6 [96]	12.4 [105]	-15.4 [117]
▲ Changeup	17.2%	83 [92]	14.6 [85]	-28.6 [97]
◇ Curveball	24.7%	79.3 [103]	-5 [90]	-42.1 [114]

Raisel Iglesias   RHP
Born: 01/04/90   Age: 31   Bats: R   Throws: R
Height: 6'2"   Weight: 190   Origin: International Free Agent, 2014

YEAR	TEAM	LVL	AGE	W	L	SV	G	GS	IP	H	HR	BB/9	K/9	K	GB%	BABIP
2018	CIN	MLB	28	2	5	30	66	0	72	52	12	3.1	10.0	80	38.6%	.234
2019	CIN	MLB	29	3	12	34	68	0	67	61	12	2.8	12.0	89	29.9%	.318
2020	CIN	MLB	30	4	3	8	22	0	23	16	1	2.0	12.1	31	38.9%	.288
2021 FS	LAA	MLB	31	2	2	32	57	0	50	41	7	3.2	11.1	61	37.3%	.288
2021 DC	LAA	MLB	31	2	2	32	57	0	57	47	8	3.2	11.1	70	37.3%	.288

Comparables: Mychal Givens, Kelvin Herrera, Jacob Barnes

Some restaurants have a signature dish that is widely known, and when you eat there you're certain it will be the best thing on the menu. At other places there are dishes you know are very, very good and rarely disappoint, but you can't help wondering if you should order something else to see if it's better. Pasta Raisel at GAB has often felt more like the latter than the former. Since moving to the bullpen during the 2016 season the lightning-armed Cuban has often been very good, but has never been quite the consistently dominant force his stuff portends. Iglesias bounced back from a subpar 2019 to post the best walk and whiff rates of his career and was only taken deep once after allowing 12 dingers in each of the previous two seasons. That last part isn't sustainable while pitching in the Cincinnati launching pad, so it's less likely Iglesias found another gear last year than there were just fewer games for his inevitable clunkers to find him. Maybe he won't need it in Anaheim.

YEAR	TEAM	LVL	AGE	WHIP	ERA	DRA-	WARP	MPH	FB%	WHF	CSP
2018	CIN	MLB	28	1.07	2.38	77	1.2	97.8	50.1%	34.0%	
2019	CIN	MLB	29	1.22	4.16	78	1.1	97.7	47.8%	33.8%	
2020	CIN	MLB	30	0.91	2.74	75	0.5	98.1	46.3%	39.0%	
2021 FS	LAA	MLB	31	1.18	3.29	78	0.9	97.8	48.0%	35.1%	47.1%
2021 DC	LAA	MLB	31	1.18	3.29	78	1.0	97.8	48.0%	35.1%	47.1%

Los Angeles Angels 2021

Raisel Iglesias, continued

Pitch Shape vs LHH

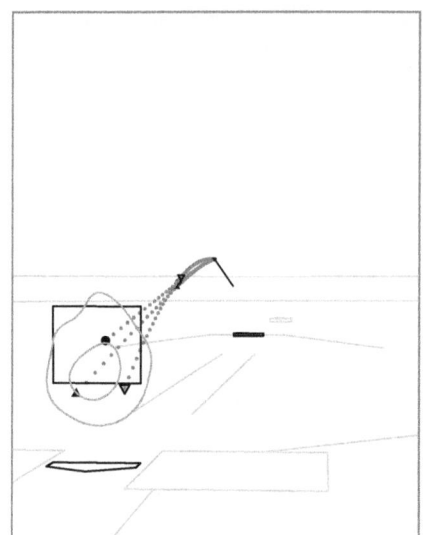

Pitch Shape vs RHH

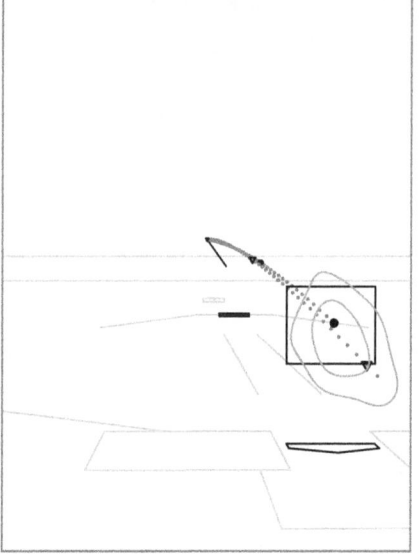

Type	Frequency	Velocity	H Movement	V Movement
● Fastball	42.5%	96.3 [112]	-8.5 [91]	-12.3 [108]
☐ Sinker	3.3%	96.8 [122]	-11.8 [109]	-14.9 [118]
▲ Changeup	20.3%	89.3 [116]	-14.5 [85]	-27.4 [100]
▽ Slider	32.9%	84.9 [104]	9 [114]	-30.9 [108]

Mike Mayers RHP

Born: 12/06/91   Age: 29   Bats: R   Throws: R
Height: 6'2"   Weight: 220   Origin: Round 3, 2013 Draft (#93 overall)

YEAR	TEAM	LVL	AGE	W	L	SV	G	GS	IP	H	HR	BB/9	K/9	K	GB%	BABIP
2018	MEM	AAA	26	0	0	3	5	0	7²	5	0	4.7	9.4	8	47.6%	.263
2018	STL	MLB	26	2	1	1	50	0	51²	59	7	2.6	8.5	49	41.6%	.344
2019	MEM	AAA	27	0	1	6	20	1	20	21	4	3.1	10.3	23	52.7%	.327
2019	STL	MLB	27	0	1	0	16	0	19	21	3	5.2	7.6	16	21.7%	.316
2020	LAA	MLB	28	2	0	2	29	0	30	18	2	2.7	12.9	43	32.4%	.242
2021 FS	LAA	MLB	29	2	2	4	57	0	50	43	7	3.1	10.0	55	37.2%	.281
2021 DC	LAA	MLB	29	2	2	4	57	0	57	49	9	3.1	10.0	63	37.2%	.281

Comparables: Drew VerHagen, Austin Brice, Casey Sadler

Following a 2019 so dreadful it got him booted out of St. Louis, Mayers bucked the trend and made 2020 his year. He added a new cutter, cribbed from an Instagram post of Mariano Rivera tracing his grip on a baseball for Roy Halladay, and by the end of the season was basically the only reliever Joe Maddon could rely upon. There was a second change, presumably spurred by a MySpace message we didn't hear about: Mayers made his slider his most-used pitch, making both of his fastballs less predictable. The reinvention elicited the best strikeout rate of Mayers' career that, unrealistically low ERA or not, cements him as the Angels' most trusted in-house relief option. Only four other pitchers reached 30 innings last year without a single start.

YEAR	TEAM	LVL	AGE	WHIP	ERA	DRA-	WARP	MPH	FB%	WHF	CSP
2018	MEM	AAA	26	1.17	0.00	73	0.1				
2018	STL	MLB	26	1.43	4.70	90	0.5	98.4	60.4%	23.2%	
2019	MEM	AAA	27	1.40	3.15	86	0.4				
2019	STL	MLB	27	1.68	6.63	164	-0.5	96.9	53.2%	29.1%	
2020	LAA	MLB	28	0.90	2.10	74	0.7	95.9	57.8%	35.7%	
2021 FS	LAA	MLB	29	1.21	3.67	86	0.6	96.8	57.6%	30.6%	45.8%
2021 DC	LAA	MLB	29	1.21	3.67	86	0.7	96.8	57.6%	30.6%	45.8%

Los Angeles Angels 2021

Mike Mayers, continued

Pitch Shape vs LHH   **Pitch Shape vs RHH**

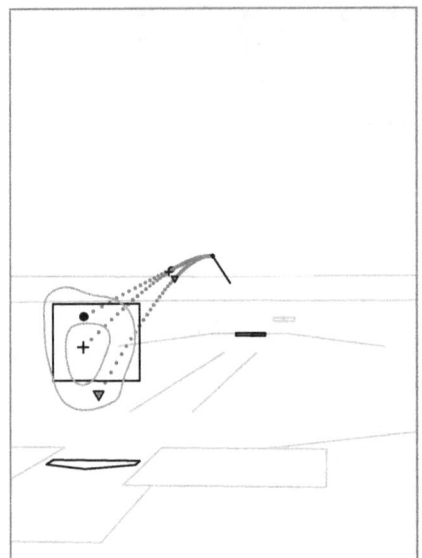
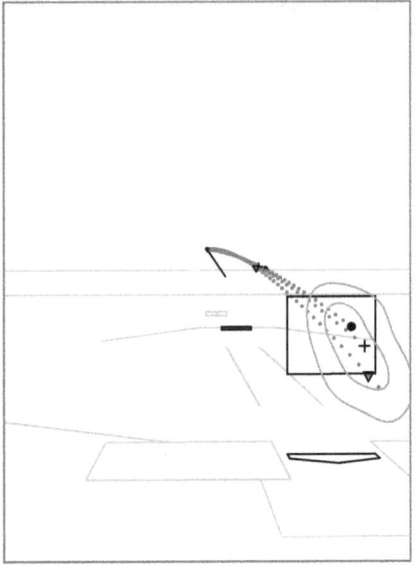

Type	Frequency	Velocity	H Movement	V Movement
● Fastball	33.4%	94.3 [105]	-9.2 [88]	-12.8 [107]
+ Cutter	24.4%	90.3 [113]	1.1 [95]	-21.7 [110]
▽ Slider	39.6%	85.3 [106]	2.8 [91]	-32.9 [102]

Felix Peña RHP

Born: 02/25/90   Age: 31   Bats: R   Throws: R
Height: 6'2"   Weight: 220   Origin: International Free Agent, 2009

YEAR	TEAM	LVL	AGE	W	L	SV	G	GS	IP	H	HR	BB/9	K/9	K	GB%	BABIP
2018	SL	AAA	28	1	2	0	10	9	33¹	30	2	4.3	10.3	38	38.6%	.346
2018	LAA	MLB	28	3	5	0	19	17	92²	87	12	2.7	8.3	85	43.0%	.290
2019	LAA	MLB	29	8	3	0	22	7	96¹	80	16	3.2	9.4	101	44.0%	.256
2020	LAA	MLB	30	3	0	2	25	0	26²	27	2	2.7	9.8	29	50.6%	.333
2021 FS	LAA	MLB	31	2	2	0	57	0	50	45	7	3.8	9.6	53	43.5%	.289
2021 DC	LAA	MLB	31	2	2	0	57	0	57	51	8	3.8	9.6	60	43.5%	.289

Comparables: Jacob Barnes, Joe Biagini, Paul Sewald

Even allowing for the "combined" qualifier, the list of starting pitchers involved in a no-hitter is a short one. The list of starting pitchers unceremoniously kicked to the bullpen the next season can't go too far beyond finger counting. In Peña's case, there was the extenuating circumstance of a torn ACL ending his 2019, with the ultimate result that he was never quite able to complete the build-up to the attenuated season. Having fallen behind, he's likely entrenched in the bullpen now barring numerous injuries in the Angels' rotation, but the culprit is less underperformance than how much the onetime marginal starter/swingman thrived in a traditional relief role. The velocity was back after a drop (preceding the injury), but the most encouraging note was a home run rate half of his major-league average. It's unlikely there's another turn towards the rotation in Peña's future, but much as combined no-hitter is sweet regardless of the modifier, a dominant relief pitcher (provided he can continue to control fly balls) is a great outcome regardless of how many times it comes via the "converted starter" route.

YEAR	TEAM	LVL	AGE	WHIP	ERA	DRA-	WARP	MPH	FB%	WHF	CSP
2018	SL	AAA	28	1.38	3.51	85	0.6				
2018	LAA	MLB	28	1.24	4.18	92	1.2	94.2	57.9%	26.0%	
2019	LAA	MLB	29	1.18	4.58	84	1.4	93.6	49.2%	29.4%	
2020	LAA	MLB	30	1.31	4.05	72	0.6	96.0	48.5%	27.8%	
2021 FS	LAA	MLB	31	1.33	4.17	94	0.4	94.3	51.1%	28.2%	46.6%
2021 DC	LAA	MLB	31	1.33	4.17	94	0.5	94.3	51.1%	28.2%	46.6%

Felix Peña, continued

Pitch Shape vs LHH	Pitch Shape vs RHH
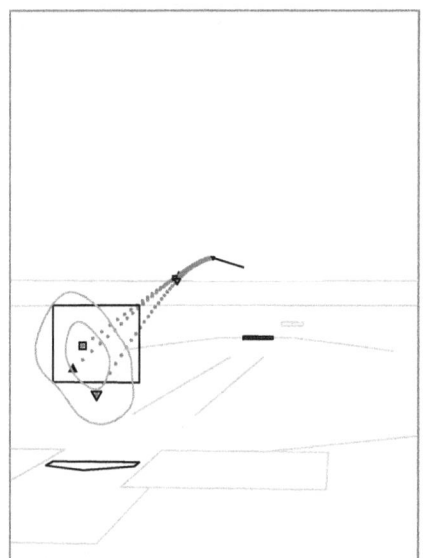	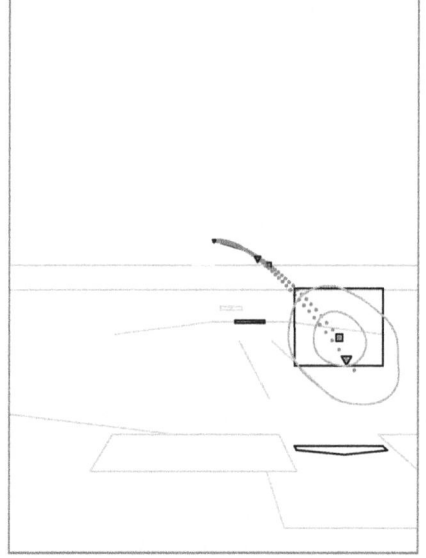

Type	Frequency	Velocity	H Movement	V Movement
● Fastball	4.1%	93.8 [104]	-11.3 [78]	-14.7 [101]
□ Sinker	44.3%	94.5 [111]	-14.4 [90]	-17.1 [111]
▲ Changeup	21.1%	86.6 [106]	-15 [82]	-26.7 [102]
▽ Slider	30.4%	84.8 [104]	-1.7 [74]	-31.5 [106]

Patrick Sandoval LHP

Born: 10/18/96   Age: 24   Bats: L   Throws: L
Height: 6'3"   Weight: 190   Origin: Round 11, 2015 Draft (#319 overall)

YEAR	TEAM	LVL	AGE	W	L	SV	G	GS	IP	H	HR	BB/9	K/9	K	GB%	BABIP
2018	QC	LO-A	21	7	1	1	14	10	65	58	4	1.5	9.8	71	45.9%	.305
2018	FAY	HI-A	21	2	0	1	5	3	23	12	1	1.6	10.2	26	46.2%	.216
2018	IE	HI-A	21	1	0	0	3	3	14^2	6	0	3.7	12.9	21	46.7%	.200
2018	MOB	AA	21	1	0	0	4	4	19^2	12	0	3.7	12.4	27	35.7%	.286
2019	MOB	AA	22	0	3	0	5	4	20	14	1	3.1	14.4	32	50.0%	.310
2019	SL	AAA	22	4	4	0	15	15	60^1	84	7	5.2	9.8	66	42.7%	.403
2019	LAA	MLB	22	0	4	0	10	9	39^1	35	6	4.3	9.6	42	45.8%	.293
2020	LAA	MLB	23	1	5	0	9	6	36^2	37	10	2.9	8.1	33	55.3%	.260
2021 FS	LAA	MLB	24	9	8	0	26	26	150	136	19	4.4	9.2	152	48.9%	.289
2021 DC	LAA	MLB	24	4	3	0	22	6	52.7	47	6	4.4	9.2	53	48.9%	.289

Comparables: Cristian Javier, Ranger Suárez, Logan Allen

We all tell ourselves little lies in the interest of self-care. "It won't affect me tomorow if I watch this next episode before bed." "I'll start eating healthier when I finish this bag of chips." "No one noticed me trip over my own feet just now." For pitchers underperforming without their stuff ghosting them, the lie is pretty uniform: "I was tipping my pitches." In some cases, it's probably true, but you never hear the story, "I was tipping my pitches and it turned out fine." More likely, it's an explanation seeking a reason, a pitcher stricken by the vagaries of a short stint putting a reason to what might be better explained as random. In any case, it was a step-back sophomore season for a starting pitcher for whom the Angels have high hopes.

YEAR	TEAM	LVL	AGE	WHIP	ERA	DRA-	WARP	MPH	FB%	WHF	CSP
2018	QC	LO-A	21	1.06	2.49	70	1.5				
2018	FAY	HI-A	21	0.70	2.74	59	0.7				
2018	IE	HI-A	21	0.82	0.00	51	0.5				
2018	MOB	AA	21	1.02	1.37	52	0.7				
2019	MOB	AA	22	1.05	3.60	52	0.6				
2019	SL	AAA	22	1.97	6.41	141	-0.1				
2019	LAA	MLB	22	1.37	5.03	89	0.6	94.8	46.5%	32.8%	
2020	LAA	MLB	23	1.34	5.65	101	0.3	94.5	44.6%	27.6%	
2021 FS	LAA	MLB	24	1.40	4.16	95	1.9	94.7	45.5%	29.9%	46.6%
2021 DC	LAA	MLB	24	1.40	4.16	95	0.6	94.7	45.5%	29.9%	46.6%

Los Angeles Angels 2021

Patrick Sandoval, continued

Pitch Shape vs LHH

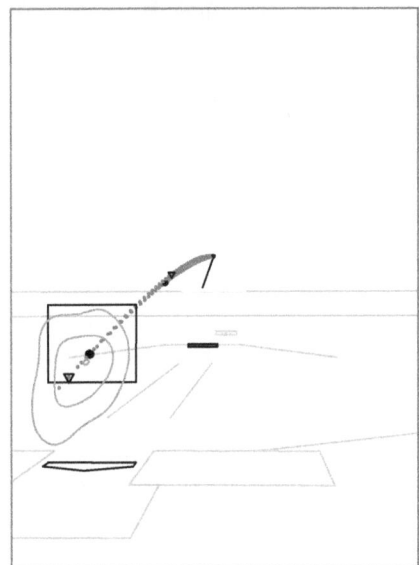

Pitch Shape vs RHH

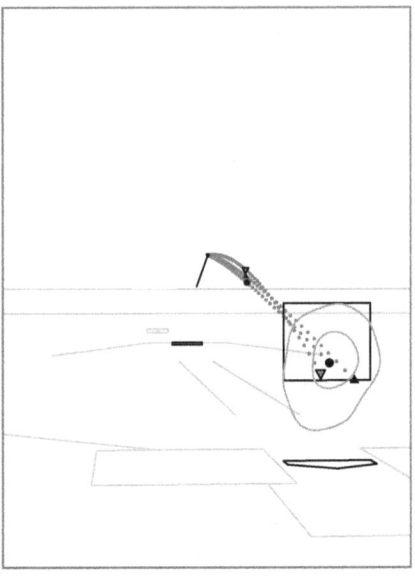

Type	Frequency	Velocity	H Movement	V Movement
● Fastball	44.6%	92.8 [101]	4.5 [111]	-14.7 [101]
▲ Changeup	23.1%	84.2 [96]	10.2 [108]	-25.9 [104]
▽ Slider	25.3%	84.7 [103]	-6 [103]	-31.8 [106]
◇ Curveball	7.0%	78.1 [98]	-6.2 [95]	-49.7 [97]

Aaron Slegers   RHP

Born: 09/04/92   Age: 28   Bats: R   Throws: R
Height: 6'10"   Weight: 260   Origin: Round 5, 2013 Draft (#140 overall)

YEAR	TEAM	LVL	AGE	W	L	SV	G	GS	IP	H	HR	BB/9	K/9	K	GB%	BABIP
2018	ROC	AAA	25	5	7	0	15	15	85^1	85	12	2.0	6.0	57	43.0%	.285
2018	MIN	MLB	25	1	1	0	4	2	13^2	17	3	1.3	4.0	6	39.2%	.292
2019	DUR	AAA	26	6	7	0	26	15	112^1	130	22	2.2	6.4	80	41.0%	.309
2019	TB	MLB	26	0	0	1	1	0	3	3	1	0.0	0.0	0	36.4%	.200
2020	TB	MLB	27	0	0	2	11	1	26	18	1	1.7	6.6	19	56.0%	.233
2021 FS	LAA	MLB	28	2	2	0	57	0	50	51	8	2.2	6.6	36	45.8%	.284
2021 DC	LAA	MLB	28	2	2	0	56	0	40	40	6	2.2	6.6	29	45.8%	.284

Comparables: Luis Perdomo, Erick Fedde, Jeff Hoffman

Hey, everyone! Thanks for checking back in. Slegers is still tall, of course, but now he looks like he's also an effective pitcher—or, at least, as effective as one can be in a pandemic-shortened season. While throwing slightly fewer fastballs in favor of more sliders, he used his height to his advantage by burying the ball in the zone, which, in turn, resulted in a groundball rate over 50 percent for the first time as a major leaguer. That proved to be beneficial for Slegers in a very obvious and meaningful way, as he allowed one home run in 2020 after permitting seven in his first 32 career innings. He should hold onto a bullpen spot for as long as he can keep the ball in play and throw multiple frames.

YEAR	TEAM	LVL	AGE	WHIP	ERA	DRA-	WARP	MPH	FB%	WHF	CSP
2018	ROC	AAA	25	1.22	3.80	112	0.0				
2018	MIN	MLB	25	1.39	5.27	133	-0.1	91.9	68.5%	15.0%	
2019	DUR	AAA	26	1.41	5.05	111	1.2				
2019	TB	MLB	26	1.00	3.00	138	0.0	91.2	66.7%	8.0%	
2020	TB	MLB	27	0.88	3.46	85	0.4	92.5	62.0%	22.4%	
2021 FS	LAA	MLB	28	1.27	4.27	99	0.3	92.4	63.2%	20.5%	48.5%
2021 DC	LAA	MLB	28	1.27	4.27	99	0.3	92.4	63.2%	20.5%	48.5%

Los Angeles Angels 2021

Aaron Slegers, continued

Pitch Shape vs LHH

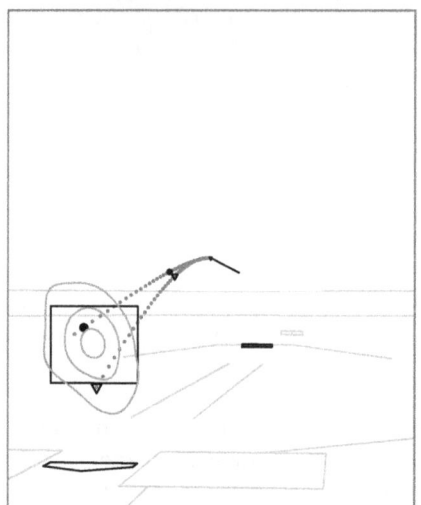

Pitch Shape vs RHH

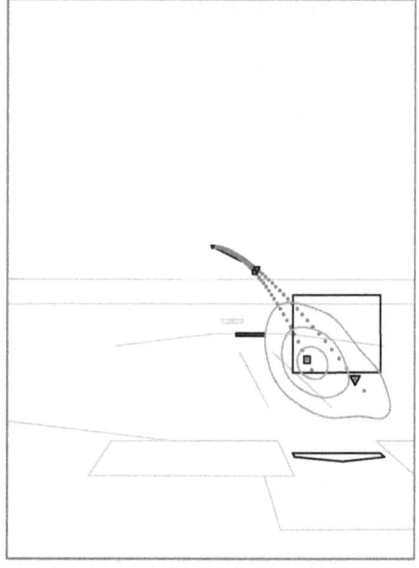

Type	Frequency	Velocity	H Movement	V Movement
● Fastball	22.8%	91.3 [96]	-5.8 [104]	-16.6 [96]
□ Sinker	38.1%	91.4 [95]	-13.8 [95]	-22.3 [94]
▲ Changeup	7.9%	86.1 [104]	-11.8 [100]	-28.6 [97]
▽ Slider	29.4%	85.1 [105]	2.2 [88]	-30.6 [109]

Julio Teheran   RHP

Born: 01/27/91   Age: 30   Bats: R   Throws: R
Height: 6'2"   Weight: 205   Origin: International Free Agent, 2007

YEAR	TEAM	LVL	AGE	W	L	SV	G	GS	IP	H	HR	BB/9	K/9	K	GB%	BABIP
2018	ATL	MLB	27	9	9	0	31	31	175^2	122	26	4.3	8.3	162	38.0%	.218
2019	ATL	MLB	28	10	11	0	33	33	174^2	148	22	4.3	8.3	162	38.7%	.270
2020	LAA	MLB	29	0	4	0	10	9	31^1	39	12	4.6	5.7	20	36.0%	.273
2021 FS	LAA	MLB	30	9	9	0	26	26	150	145	25	4.1	7.8	130	38.3%	.282
2021 DC	LAA	MLB	30	2	2	0	8	8	40.3	39	6	4.1	7.8	35	38.3%	.282

Comparables: Jonathon Niese, Jake Odorizzi, Kevin Gausman

An adaption of Henry James' novella *The Turn of the Screw* caught everyone's attention in the latter half of 2020, giving everyone the Halloween scares the rest of the world had just been in too-scant supply of. What's *The Haunting of Bly Manor*? We were referring to Teheran's 2020, the real haunted house story. The velocity has been in decline for a while, and that trend continued, but no one could have prepared for the newly-made Angel to accumulate a number of home runs equal to sixty percent of his strikeout total. The DRA doubling makes a bit more sense in that light. Beyond tamping down homers, Teheran will need to regain his old control if he's to make his abysmal season a memory. Even if he can, he's as likely to remember the season as *The Turn of the Screw*'s storyteller: "'Nothing but the impression. I took that *here*'—he tapped his heart. 'I've never lost it.'"

YEAR	TEAM	LVL	AGE	WHIP	ERA	DRA-	WARP	MPH	FB%	WHF	CSP
2018	ATL	MLB	27	1.17	3.94	90	2.5	92.4	61.9%	28.5%	
2019	ATL	MLB	28	1.32	3.81	94	2.2	91.8	63.8%	22.2%	
2020	LAA	MLB	29	1.76	10.05	191	-1.2	91.3	60.3%	14.6%	
2021 FS	LAA	MLB	30	1.42	4.88	110	0.6	91.9	62.7%	22.6%	45.1%
2021 DC	LAA	MLB	30	1.42	4.88	110	0.2	91.9	62.7%	22.6%	45.1%

Los Angeles Angels 2021

Julio Teheran, continued

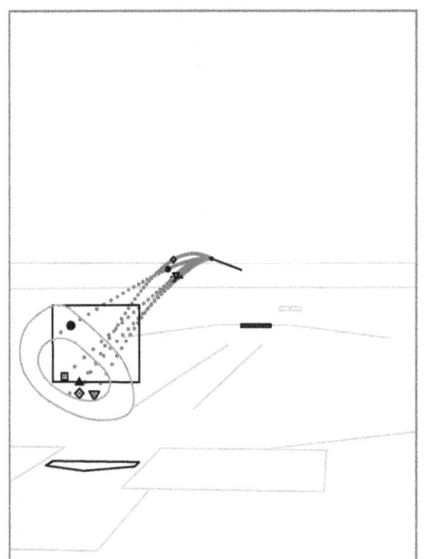
Pitch Shape vs LHH

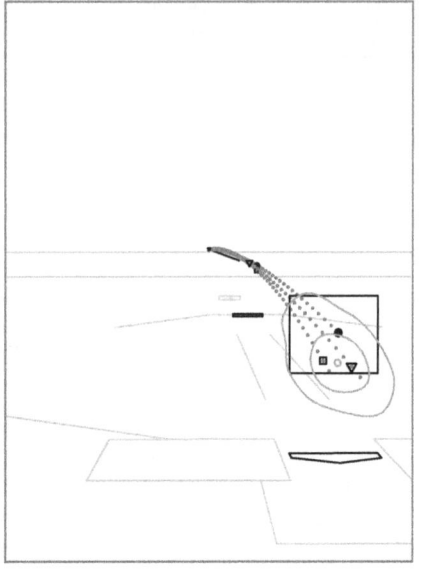
Pitch Shape vs RHH

Type	Frequency	Velocity	H Movement	V Movement
● Fastball	26.0%	89.2 [89]	-7 [99]	-18.7 [90]
☐ Sinker	34.3%	88.8 [81]	-14.4 [90]	-26.8 [80]
▲ Changeup	11.2%	82.1 [88]	-13.4 [91]	-28.8 [96]
▽ Slider	19.2%	80.9 [86]	3.5 [93]	-34.4 [98]
◇ Curveball	9.3%	72.3 [75]	11.3 [115]	-50.8 [95]

PLAYER COMMENTS WITHOUT GRAPHS

Jordyn Adams   CF
Born: 10/18/99   Age: 21   Bats: R   Throws: R
Height: 6'2"   Weight: 180   Origin: Round 1, 2018 Draft (#17 overall)

YEAR	TEAM	LVL	AGE	PA	R	2B	3B	HR	RBI	BB	K	SB	CS	AVG/OBP/SLG
2018	ANG	ROK	18	82	8	2	2	0	5	10	23	5	2	.243/.354/.329
2018	ORM	ROK	18	40	5	4	1	0	8	4	7	0	1	.314/.375/.486
2019	ANG	ROK	19	14	4	1	0	0	4	1	3	4	0	.538/.571/.615
2019	BUR	LO-A	19	428	52	15	2	7	31	50	94	12	5	.250/.346/.358
2019	IE	HI-A	19	40	7	1	1	1	1	5	14	0	1	.229/.325/.400
2021 FS	LAA	MLB	21	600	48	22	3	9	52	41	200	4	3	.202/.263/.306

Comparables: Aaron Hicks, Kyle Tucker, Slade Heathcott

Speaking about Adams' approach to games, fellow high-upside, eye-catching tools prospect Brandon Marsh described him as "like a caged bird that just got released, like a gazelle or something that can fly." This raises several questions—about the non-avian taxonomy of gazelles, about whether Marsh could name a species of bird if asked, about what kinds of birds Marsh has seen in what sorts of cages—but in any case the simile illustrates the explosive, immediate potential Adams evidences to scouts and casual watchers alike. It seems eminently possible in a year or so Marsh hands off the top prospect reins to ~~something that can fly~~ Adams, provided the high school two-sport star is able to continue advancing his bat in a more normal season of reps.

YEAR	TEAM	LVL	AGE	PA	DRC+	BABIP	BRR	FRAA	WARP
2018	ANG	ROK	18	82		.362			
2018	ORM	ROK	18	40		.379			
2019	ANG	ROK	19	14		.700			
2019	BUR	LO-A	19	428	122	.316	2.4	CF(73): -1.2, LF(9): 2.5, RF(8): -0.4	2.6
2019	IE	HI-A	19	40	94	.350	0.2	CF(4): 0.4, LF(2): -0.3, RF(2): -0.3	0.1
2021 FS	LAA	MLB	21	600	56	.297	0.0	CF 4, LF 1	-1.0

Los Angeles Angels 2021

Franklin Barreto 2B
Born: 02/27/96 Age: 25 Bats: R Throws: R
Height: 5'10" Weight: 208 Origin: International Free Agent, 2012

YEAR	TEAM	LVL	AGE	PA	R	2B	3B	HR	RBI	BB	K	SB	CS	AVG/OBP/SLG
2018	NAS	AAA	22	333	54	16	1	18	46	39	106	5	2	.259/.357/.514
2018	OAK	MLB	22	75	10	4	0	5	16	1	29	0	0	.233/.253/.493
2019	LV	AAA	23	424	88	29	5	19	65	42	113	15	1	.295/.374/.552
2019	OAK	MLB	23	58	6	2	0	2	5	1	23	1	0	.123/.138/.263
2020	LAA	MLB	24	18	0	0	0	0	2	0	8	1	0	.118/.167/.118
2020	OAK	MLB	24	10	5	0	0	0	0	0	7	0	0	.000/.000/.000
2021 FS	LAA	MLB	25	600	70	23	2	20	70	42	219	8	3	.211/.278/.378
2021 DC	LAA	MLB	25	127	14	5	0	4	15	8	46	1	1	.211/.278/.378

Comparables: Isan Díaz, Josh VanMeter, Scott Kingery

Barreto's trade deadline acquisition meant the book officially closed on the Josh Donaldson trade, with the A's having received a penultimate season of Brett Lawrie, 219 plate appearances from Barreto over four seasons, and Tommy La Stella for September and seven October games. The apparently inequitable swap smarts even more given the strange usage the A's elected for Barreto, who has played between 21 and 32 major-league games in each of the past four seasons. The .549 OPS makes that choice hard to dispute, but it's nevertheless about as suboptimal a path one could design for getting a player comfortable at the major league level. It's a six-month soft launch, with no grand opening in sight—not a venture being set up for success. With Barreto having appeared at four defensive positions in the majors and the Angels lacking much in the way of versatility, they have little reason not to give the still-somehow-young infielder an extended look.

YEAR	TEAM	LVL	AGE	PA	DRC+	BABIP	BRR	FRAA	WARP
2018	NAS	AAA	22	333	128	.337	3.5	2B(60): -2.2, SS(11): 0.4	1.9
2018	OAK	MLB	22	75	76	.308	-1.1	2B(26): -1.7, SS(2): -0.0	-0.3
2019	LV	AAA	23	424	108	.374	2.2	2B(47): -5.1, SS(30): 0.1, 3B(9): 0.8	1.8
2019	OAK	MLB	23	58	50	.156	0.5	2B(17): -0.2, SS(5): -0.2	-0.1
2020	LAA	MLB	24	18	49	.222	-0.1	2B(2): 0.2, 3B(2): 0.1, SS(1): -0.1	0.0
2020	OAK	MLB	24	10	40	.000	0.0	2B(4): 0.2, SS(3): -0.0	0.0
2021 FS	LAA	MLB	25	600	77	.308	0.3	2B -1, 3B 0	0.0
2021 DC	LAA	MLB	25	127	77	.308	0.1	2B 0	0.0

Jose Miguel Fernandez 1B

Born: 04/27/88 Age: 33 Bats: L Throws: R
Height: 5'10" Weight: 185 Origin:

YEAR	TEAM	LVL	AGE	PA	R	2B	3B	HR	RBI	BB	K	SB	CS	AVG/OBP/SLG
2018	SL	AAA	30	394	66	19	1	17	59	33	34	2	2	.333/.396/.535
2018	LAA	MLB	30	123	9	8	0	2	11	6	14	1	0	.267/.309/.388
2019	DOO	KBO	31	645	87	34	0	15	88	61	54	1	2	.344/.409/.483
2020	DOO	KBO	32	668	104	29	0	21	105	58	42	0	1	.340/.404/.497
2021								No projection						

Comparables: Johnny Giavotella, Luis Antonio Rodriguez, Edgar Gonzalez

If you're looking to pull an elaborate heist in Seoul and need some video to patch into the closed circuit feed to fool the security guard, there's no better choice than Doosan's DH, flicking infinite liners into the hole for base hits. One of three Jose Fernandezes to appear in a big league game last decade, Jose Miguel has settled in to life in Korea as the league's Edgar Martinez. The batting title has narrowly eluded his grasp two years running, but after consecutive .340 campaigns, it's only a matter of time. He can't run and he's the only international player who doesn't play defense, but none of that matters here, as he's one of the five or so best hitters in the league.

YEAR	TEAM	LVL	AGE	PA	DRC+	BABIP	BRR	FRAA	WARP
2018	SL	AAA	30	394	137	.333	-0.7	2B(33): 1.4, 1B(17): 1.9, 3B(16): -1.0	2.2
2018	LAA	MLB	30	123	97	.290	-2.5	1B(28): -3.0, 3B(2): -0.1, 2B(1): 0.0	-0.4
2019	DOO	KBO	31	645					
2020	DOO	KBO	32	668					
2021							No projection		

Robel García 2B

Born: 03/28/93 Age: 28 Bats: S Throws: R
Height: 6'0" Weight: 195 Origin: International Free Agent, 2010

YEAR	TEAM	LVL	AGE	PA	R	2B	3B	HR	RBI	BB	K	SB	CS	AVG/OBP/SLG
2019	TNS	AA	26	92	12	5	0	6	26	12	22	1	1	.295/.391/.590
2019	IOW	AAA	26	296	51	12	2	21	52	30	98	3	3	.281/.361/.585
2019	CHC	MLB	26	80	8	2	2	5	11	7	35	0	0	.208/.275/.500
2021 FS	LAA	MLB	28	600	72	20	2	21	70	52	225	0	0	.201/.279/.371
2021 DC	LAA	MLB	28	34	4	1	0	1	3	2	12	0	0	.201/.279/.371

Comparables: David Bote, Mitch Walding, Jai Miller

García has serious power for a second baseman but has to sell out so fully to reach it that even Gene Simmons gives him the side eye.

Los Angeles Angels 2021

YEAR	TEAM	LVL	AGE	PA	DRC+	BABIP	BRR	FRAA	WARP
2019	TNS	AA	26	92	171	.333	-0.7	3B(18): 0.4, 2B(4): 0.6, SS(1): -0.0	1.1
2019	IOW	AAA	26	296	125	.364	2.8	2B(29): 0.8, LF(21): 2.9, 3B(19): -2.3	2.1
2019	CHC	MLB	26	80	71	.303	-0.4	2B(18): -1.0, LF(5): -0.2, RF(1): -0.1	-0.2
2021 FS	LAA	MLB	28	600	75	.296	-0.6	2B -2, 1B 0	-0.7
2021 DC	LAA	MLB	28	34	75	.296	0.0	2B 0	0.0

Jeremiah Jackson SS
Born: 03/26/00   Age: 21   Bats: R   Throws: R
Height: 6'0"   Weight: 165   Origin: Round 2, 2018 Draft (#57 overall)

YEAR	TEAM	LVL	AGE	PA	R	2B	3B	HR	RBI	BB	K	SB	CS	AVG/OBP/SLG
2018	ORM	ROK	18	100	13	6	3	2	9	8	34	4	1	.198/.260/.396
2018	ANG	ROK	18	91	13	4	2	5	14	7	25	6	1	.317/.374/.598
2019	ORM	ROK+	19	287	47	14	2	23	60	23	96	5	1	.265/.331/.609
2021 FS	LAA	MLB	21	600	40	17	3	9	46	32	256	3	2	.157/.209/.249

Another player whose future is clouded by the lack of 2020 data, there's a lot we don't know about Jackson: Can he stick at shortstop as his frame fills out? Is striking out a third of the time to be expected, moving forward? Most importantly, how much of the Pioneer League-record tying home run power is real? He can move well and has a strong arm, so sliding over to second or third wouldn't be a huge long-term concern to his viability given the showcase he put on in Rookie ball. Really, the biggest red flag for Jackson given the system in which he's developing is that he's not an outfielder, the only position which the Angels seem interested in developing.

YEAR	TEAM	LVL	AGE	PA	DRC+	BABIP	BRR	FRAA	WARP
2018	ORM	ROK	18	100		.286			
2018	ANG	ROK	18	91		.396			
2019	ORM	ROK+	19	287		.314			
2021 FS	LAA	MLB	21	600	23	.267	0.3	SS -5, 2B 0	-4.7

D'Shawn Knowles OF
Born: 01/16/01   Age: 20   Bats: S   Throws: R
Height: 6'0"   Weight: 165   Origin: International Free Agent, 2017

YEAR	TEAM	LVL	AGE	PA	R	2B	3B	HR	RBI	BB	K	SB	CS	AVG/OBP/SLG
2018	ANG	ROK	17	130	19	4	1	1	14	15	27	7	4	.301/.385/.381
2018	ORM	ROK	17	123	27	9	2	4	15	13	38	2	3	.321/.398/.550
2019	ORM	ROK+	18	286	38	11	4	6	28	25	76	5	4	.244/.311/.392
2021 FS	LAA	MLB	20	600	43	18	3	8	47	38	221	5	4	.184/.240/.272

The year Beyoncé Knowles was 19, her group Destiny's Child released *Survivor*, one of the seminal albums of the 2000s, and Beyoncé went solo, launching perhaps the most successful pop career of all time. As with so many other players, the outfielder Knowles found himself on the sidelines in 2020, missing a chance to make his own age-19 year something great. Much like Beyoncé, though, Knowles began to untether himself from another act with whom he's often been associated (fellow Angels 2017 Bahamian glove-and-speed outfielder Trent Deveaux), a higher offensive ceiling drawing more attention his way. It's a crowded Angels outfield, both at the majors and below, but entering a crowded space didn't ever slow down Beyoncé.

YEAR	TEAM	LVL	AGE	PA	DRC+	BABIP	BRR	FRAA	WARP
2018	ANG	ROK	17	130		.384			
2018	ORM	ROK	17	123		.463			
2019	ORM	ROK+	18	286		.312			
2021 FS	LAA	MLB	20	600	39	.288	0.4	CF 0, RF -1	-3.4

Juan Lagares CF
Born: 03/17/89   Age: 32   Bats: R   Throws: R
Height: 6'2"   Weight: 219   Origin: International Free Agent, 2006

YEAR	TEAM	LVL	AGE	PA	R	2B	3B	HR	RBI	BB	K	SB	CS	AVG/OBP/SLG
2018	NYM	MLB	29	64	9	1	1	0	6	3	9	3	1	.339/.375/.390
2019	NYM	MLB	30	285	38	12	1	5	27	22	75	4	1	.213/.279/.326
2020	NYM	MLB	31	0	0	0	0	0	0	0	0	0	0	None/None/None
2021 FS	LAA	MLB	32	600	53	25	2	12	58	35	142	11	5	.231/.285/.353

Comparables: Pete Whisenant, Randy Kutcher, John Shelby

The former all-world gloveman briefly escaped from Queens to sunny San Diego, but couldn't find purchase either with the Padres or in a brief reunion with the Mets. Now seven years removed from his Gold Glove, teams would rather employ younger, faster, and cheaper center fielders who also can't hit.

Los Angeles Angels 2021

YEAR	TEAM	LVL	AGE	PA	DRC+	BABIP	BRR	FRAA	WARP
2018	NYM	MLB	29	64	88	.392	1.0	CF(20): 1.5	0.4
2019	NYM	MLB	30	285	61	.279	3.3	CF(125): -5.7	-0.6
2020	NYM	MLB	31	0				CF(2): 0.1	
2021 FS	LAA	MLB	32	600	73	.289	0.7	CF -2	-0.4

Kevin Maitan 3B
Born: 02/12/00 Age: 21 Bats: S Throws: R
Height: 6'2" Weight: 190 Origin: International Free Agent, 2016

YEAR	TEAM	LVL	AGE	PA	R	2B	3B	HR	RBI	BB	K	SB	CS	AVG/OBP/SLG
2018	ORM	ROK	18	284	42	13	1	8	26	19	66	1	2	.248/.306/.397
2019	BUR	LO-A	19	532	56	11	3	12	46	39	164	7	4	.214/.278/.323
2021 FS	LAA	MLB	21	600	44	20	2	10	50	31	225	1	1	.185/.232/.283

Comparables: Dustin Peterson, Alex Liddi, Michael Chavis

Still 20 at the time of this book's publication, it'd be beyond premature to say it's too late for Maitan. You'd be forgiven the mistake, however, given how thoroughly he's been forgotten amidst a middling farm system. Just two years after he was declared a free agent and the Angels gave him a $2.2 million bonus (itself two years after an original $4.25 million bonus), Maitan was left exposed to the Rule 5 draft. There's still time for a major leaguer to emerge, but chances of Maitan regaining his prospect luster are about as strong as of him moving back to shortstop.

YEAR	TEAM	LVL	AGE	PA	DRC+	BABIP	BRR	FRAA	WARP
2018	ORM	ROK	18	284		.303			
2019	BUR	LO-A	19	532	68	.295	-1.9	3B(92): -6.9, 2B(21): -2.8	-1.4
2021 FS	LAA	MLB	21	600	39	.286	-0.5	3B -2, SS -1	-3.9

Brandon Marsh CF

Born: 12/18/97   Age: 23   Bats: L   Throws: R
Height: 6'4"   Weight: 215   Origin: Round 2, 2016 Draft (#60 overall)

YEAR	TEAM	LVL	AGE	PA	R	2B	3B	HR	RBI	BB	K	SB	CS	AVG/OBP/SLG
2018	BUR	LO-A	20	154	26	12	1	3	24	21	40	4	0	.295/.390/.470
2018	IE	HI-A	20	426	59	15	6	7	46	52	118	10	4	.256/.348/.385
2019	MOB	AA	21	412	48	21	2	7	43	47	92	18	5	.300/.383/.428
2021 FS	LAA	MLB	23	600	69	23	3	13	63	46	194	6	3	.221/.286/.351
2021 DC	LAA	MLB	23	33	3	1	0	0	3	2	10	0	0	.221/.286/.351

Comparables: Michael Saunders, Jordan Schafer, Chris Young

For all the accusations of organizational rudderlessness that have dogged the Angels for a decade, the organization's preferences in the draft have remained consistent—shoot for high-upside hitters, especially outfielders, who can contribute positively with all five tools. When you have a Mike Trout hammer, all you see are fish nails, apparently. Marsh hasn't quite gotten there with the power yet, and the lost year of development smarts here especially. Without the morass of 2020, he might have had a chance to work out his issues in the big leagues; it's not the common prospect who ascends to the top spot in an organization without ever breaking double-digit homers at a minor-league stop. The defensive reputation is that good; even if the Angels outfield is bogged down already, Marsh's glove makes room for itself. The demands of the major-league roster meant that by the end of 2020, he was taking reps at first base at the Angels alternate site in Long Beach—an unexpected turn for the player who might one day push Mike Trout to an outfield corner.

YEAR	TEAM	LVL	AGE	PA	DRC+	BABIP	BRR	FRAA	WARP
2018	BUR	LO-A	20	154	136	.400	2.9	CF(14): 1.2, RF(13): -1.3, LF(6): 0.7	1.2
2018	IE	HI-A	20	426	107	.356	4.3	CF(50): -0.8, RF(33): 3.0, LF(7): 0.5	1.1
2019	MOB	AA	21	412	141	.384	2.6	CF(55): -0.7, RF(19): 1.8, LF(13): -3.0	2.9
2021 FS	LAA	MLB	23	600	74	.315	0.3	CF 5, LF 0	0.2
2021 DC	LAA	MLB	23	33	74	.315	0.0	CF 0	0.0

Los Angeles Angels 2021

Orlando Martinez RF
Born: 02/17/98 Age: 23 Bats: L Throws: L
Height: 6'0" Weight: 185 Origin: International Free Agent, 2017

YEAR	TEAM	LVL	AGE	PA	R	2B	3B	HR	RBI	BB	K	SB	CS	AVG/OBP/SLG
2018	ORM	ROK	20	53	11	5	0	2	10	4	9	3	2	.375/.415/.604
2018	BUR	LO-A	20	238	27	12	1	3	25	17	56	6	5	.289/.340/.394
2019	IE	HI-A	21	422	55	21	4	12	49	36	79	5	4	.263/.325/.434
2021 FS	LAA	MLB	23	600	53	24	2	13	59	36	172	3	2	.222/.272/.348

Comparables: César Puello, Kirk Nieuwenhuis, Jake Cave

With an organizational outfield depth chart littered with athletic players worth keeping an eye or two on, Martinez is the underdog of the brood. Lacking a marketable skill but capable of contributing a little bit of everything, his best bet is probably to pray to David DeJesus, the patron saint of the 50 OFP, and hope that he can get enough time as a fourth outfielder to prove himself worthy of being a third.

YEAR	TEAM	LVL	AGE	PA	DRC+	BABIP	BRR	FRAA	WARP
2018	ORM	ROK	20	53		.421			
2018	BUR	LO-A	20	238	106	.373	-1.2	RF(20): 1.9, LF(18): -1.0, CF(13): 0.3	0.4
2019	IE	HI-A	21	422	110	.299	1.4	CF(41): 3.4, RF(21): -2.2, LF(20): 1.6	1.9
2021 FS	LAA	MLB	23	600	69	.295	-0.4	CF 6, LF 2	0.2

Kyren Paris SS
Born: 11/11/01 Age: 19 Bats: R Throws: R
Height: 6'0" Weight: 165 Origin: Round 2, 2019 Draft (#55 overall)

YEAR	TEAM	LVL	AGE	PA	R	2B	3B	HR	RBI	BB	K	SB	CS	AVG/OBP/SLG
2019	ANG	ROK	17	13	4	1	0	0	2	3	4	0	0	.300/.462/.400
2021 FS	LAA	MLB	19	600	41	17	2	7	45	36	238	3	2	.169/.225/.251

Comparables: Michael Chavis, Travis Demeritte, Jay Bruce

Late in 2020, the Netflix Twitter account, promoting the platform's hit series *Emily in Paris,* took to Twitter to clarify that Kyren Paris is actually meant to be pronounced with a French accent—Kyren Pah-ree (so it rhymes). The research shows all sorts of benefits to taking players who are young for their draft class—like Paris, 17 at the time of his selection—but it's less clear how those benefits manifest when they hardly play the following two seasons due to a broken hamate bone and an international pandemic. Paris still carries plenty of promise, thanks to ha versatile defensive skillset that could allow the Angels to spread him across the field like a creamy brie. The only question is how much the baguette-like crunch of lost development time will cost the not-quite-as-young prospect.

YEAR	TEAM	LVL	AGE	PA	DRC+	BABIP	BRR	FRAA	WARP
2019	ANG	ROK	17	13		.500			
2021 FS	LAA	MLB	19	600	31	.277	-0.1	SS -3	-3.8

Matt Thaiss 1B
Born: 05/06/95   Age: 26   Bats: L   Throws: R
Height: 6'0"   Weight: 215   Origin: Round 1, 2016 Draft (#16 overall)

YEAR	TEAM	LVL	AGE	PA	R	2B	3B	HR	RBI	BB	K	SB	CS	AVG/OBP/SLG
2018	MOB	AA	23	176	24	10	2	6	25	16	35	2	1	.287/.352/.490
2018	SL	AAA	23	400	54	24	6	10	51	28	68	6	3	.277/.328/.457
2019	SL	AAA	24	372	63	17	2	14	49	59	64	1	0	.274/.390/.477
2019	LAA	MLB	24	164	17	7	0	8	23	17	52	0	0	.211/.293/.422
2020	LAA	MLB	25	25	3	0	0	1	1	4	8	0	0	.143/.280/.286
2021 FS	LAA	MLB	26	600	78	23	2	20	70	62	158	0	1	.221/.308/.390
2021 DC	LAA	MLB	26	66	8	2	0	2	7	6	17	0	0	.221/.308/.390

Comparables: Ronald Guzmán, Ryan Garko, Chris Duncan

In eight 2020 games, Thaiss appeared twice at first base, twice at DH, once at second, once at third, once in left field, and once as a pinch runner. You could call it versatility, in the same sense that you could use Spam to make a hundred different meals, but you probably wouldn't want to. Like canned meat, Thaiss isn't particularly essential at any position or meal; but also like canned meat, he'll be around just about forever, in the back of the pantry, just in case.

YEAR	TEAM	LVL	AGE	PA	DRC+	BABIP	BRR	FRAA	WARP
2018	MOB	AA	23	176	123	.331	-1.1	1B(36): 2.6	0.5
2018	SL	AAA	23	400	94	.314	0.2	1B(77): 5.4	0.3
2019	SL	AAA	24	372	108	.303	1.3	3B(47): -2.5, 1B(23): -1.4	1.2
2019	LAA	MLB	24	164	91	.264	-1.6	3B(43): -3.5, 1B(13): 0.5	-0.1
2020	LAA	MLB	25	25	87	.167	-0.3	1B(2): -0.2, 2B(1): 0.2, 3B(1): -0.0	0.0
2021 FS	LAA	MLB	26	600	89	.276	-0.6	LF -4, 1B 1	-0.2
2021 DC	LAA	MLB	26	66	89	.276	-0.1	LF 0, 1B 0	0.0

Los Angeles Angels 2021

Luke Bard RHP
Born: 11/13/90 Age: 30 Bats: R Throws: R
Height: 6'3" Weight: 200 Origin: Round 1, 2012 Draft (#42 overall)

YEAR	TEAM	LVL	AGE	W	L	SV	G	GS	IP	H	HR	BB/9	K/9	K	GB%	BABIP
2018	ROC	AAA	27	3	3	1	32	0	48^1	54	6	3.4	9.7	52	34.8%	.358
2018	LAA	MLB	27	0	0	0	8	0	11^2	10	4	3.9	10.0	13	31.2%	.214
2019	SL	AAA	28	2	4	1	16	1	19	28	4	4.7	12.3	26	31.6%	.453
2019	LAA	MLB	28	3	3	0	32	3	49	41	8	2.4	7.3	40	36.9%	.248
2020	LAA	MLB	29	0	0	0	6	0	5^1	7	2	0.0	11.8	7	18.8%	.357
2021 FS	LAA	MLB	30	2	2	0	57	0	50	47	9	3.2	9.3	51	34.3%	.289
2021 DC	LAA	MLB	30	2	2	0	46	0	34	32	6	3.2	9.3	35	34.3%	.289

Comparables: Nick Wittgren, Shawn Armstrong, Mike Morin

If this Bard is Shakespeare, he's one of the lesser-known works—nothing objectionable, or tragic, certainly, just nothing you'd be likely to see at the theater (when that was still a thing). It feels cruel, in this context, to choose *Comedy of Errors*, but few managers have likely felt, with Bard on the mound, *All's Well That Ends Well*.

YEAR	TEAM	LVL	AGE	WHIP	ERA	DRA-	WARP	MPH	FB%	WHF	CSP
2018	ROC	AAA	27	1.49	4.66	87	0.4				
2018	LAA	MLB	27	1.29	5.40	152	-0.3	93.9	55.4%	20.6%	
2019	SL	AAA	28	2.00	7.11	139	-0.1				
2019	LAA	MLB	28	1.10	4.78	98	0.3	96.0	44.1%	28.7%	
2020	LAA	MLB	29	1.31	6.75	100	0.0	95.8	45.6%	33.3%	
2021 FS	LAA	MLB	30	1.31	4.48	101	0.2	95.8	45.5%	28.4%	47.0%
2021 DC	LAA	MLB	30	1.31	4.48	101	0.2	95.8	45.5%	28.4%	47.0%

Reid Detmers   LHP
Born: 07/08/99   Age: 21   Bats: L   Throws: L
Height: 6'2"   Weight: 210   Origin: Round 1, 2020 Draft (#10 overall)

   The Angels' first pitcher selected in the first round since 2014, Detmers immediately moved into their top echelon of prospects and fills in the "name like a senator from a Southern state who you always forget" hole in the system. He's also a dearly-needed arm, and a lefty at that. With "polish" atop every scouting report, a strong performance at the alternate site created some buzz that Detmers was ready for his debut last year. While the velocity merely spans the low 90s, a relatively complete four-pitch mix never had trouble eliciting punchouts at Louisville, especially as he tinkered with a new grip on an old slider that gave the pitch some healthy bite. It's the oversized curveball that marks the arsenal, however, a pitch that demands attention from the batter and speeds up his harder pitches. An aggressive assignment is likely given the Angels' perennial need of starters, so that role, like his slider, is just a matter of the quality of his grip.

Aaron Hernandez   RHP
Born: 12/02/96   Age: 24   Bats: R   Throws: R
Height: 6'1"   Weight: 170   Origin: Round 3, 2018 Draft (#93 overall)

YEAR	TEAM	LVL	AGE	W	L	SV	G	GS	IP	H	HR	BB/9	K/9	K	GB%	BABIP
2019	IE	HI-A	22	1	4	0	20	15	72^2	75	6	5.7	10.0	81	38.6%	.354
2021 FS	LAA	MLB	24	2	3	0	57	0	50	47	8	6.6	8.3	46	37.0%	.286

Comparables: Randy Rosario, Daniel Moskos, Justin Dunn

   One of those starting pitching prospects widely expected to eventually transition to relief—inconsistent, sometimes marginal velocity; spotty track record of turns through a rotation; lots of walks—Hernandez's 2020 might have been offered a ruling had he been able to take the mound. Now, the lack of clarity on his future remains, with the added complication of a path that will be chosen for him *in absentia*.

YEAR	TEAM	LVL	AGE	WHIP	ERA	DRA-	WARP	MPH	FB%	WHF	CSP
2019	IE	HI-A	22	1.67	4.46	124	-1.0				
2021 FS	LAA	MLB	24	1.69	5.82	125	-0.5				

Packy Naughton LHP

Born: 04/16/96 Age: 25 Bats: R Throws: L
Height: 6'2" Weight: 195 Origin: Round 9, 2017 Draft (#257 overall)

YEAR	TEAM	LVL	AGE	W	L	SV	G	GS	IP	H	HR	BB/9	K/9	K	GB%	BABIP
2018	DAY	LO-A	22	5	10	0	28	28	154	168	12	2.0	8.0	137	38.3%	.344
2019	DAY	HI-A	23	5	2	0	9	9	51^1	49	2	1.6	8.8	50	43.6%	.320
2019	CHA	AA	23	6	10	0	19	19	105^2	109	8	2.2	6.9	81	39.1%	.309
2021 FS	LAA	MLB	25	2	2	0	57	0	50	49	7	3.2	7.1	39	37.8%	.282

Comparables: Nick Margevicius, Josh Fleming, Yohander Méndez

With a name like a Flannery O'Connor character and a fifth-starter ceiling, Naughton came to town along with PTBNL Jose Salvador in the deadline deal that sent Brian Goodwin to the Reds. The outfielder was non-tendered by Cincinnati just months later and Naughton was left unprotected ahead of the Rule 5 deadline, reminding everyone that, much like an O'Connor story, sometimes nobody wins.

YEAR	TEAM	LVL	AGE	WHIP	ERA	DRA-	WARP	MPH	FB%	WHF	CSP
2018	DAY	LO-A	22	1.31	4.03	99	1.1				
2019	DAY	HI-A	23	1.13	2.63	86	0.5				
2019	CHA	AA	23	1.28	3.66	100	0.1				
2021 FS	LAA	MLB	25	1.34	4.27	101	0.2				

Oliver Ortega RHP

Born: 10/02/96 Age: 24 Bats: R Throws: R
Height: 6'0" Weight: 165 Origin: International Free Agent, 2015

YEAR	TEAM	LVL	AGE	W	L	SV	G	GS	IP	H	HR	BB/9	K/9	K	GB%	BABIP
2018	BUR	LO-A	21	4	5	0	19	18	82	64	6	4.5	9.4	86	32.7%	.276
2019	IE	HI-A	22	4	5	2	21	16	94^1	67	8	4.7	11.5	121	43.9%	.277
2019	MOB	AA	22	0	3	0	5	5	16^2	23	0	4.3	7.6	14	50.8%	.390
2021 FS	LAA	MLB	24	2	3	0	57	0	50	45	7	5.7	8.8	48	43.8%	.279

Comparables: Beau Burrows, Albert Abreu, Jarlin García

Mid-90s velocity that can get up to 99; a 12-to-6 curveball that combines with the heat to get healthy strikeout totals; an inconsistent delivery that results in equally healthy walk rates; a third pitch that isn't really, yet—if you're reading all that and mentally slotting Ortega into the Angels bullpen of 2022, the only rebuttal would be that the Angels *really* need to develop a starting pitcher with some upside. Perhaps a wandering hermit will happen by Salt Lake and pass on, via oral tradition, the ancient lost secrets of the changeup.

YEAR	TEAM	LVL	AGE	WHIP	ERA	DRA-	WARP	MPH	FB%	WHF	CSP
2018	BUR	LO-A	21	1.28	3.51	98	0.6				
2019	IE	HI-A	22	1.23	3.34	70	1.7				
2019	MOB	AA	22	1.86	8.64	138	-0.4				
2021 FS	LAA	MLB	24	1.54	4.95	111	-0.1				

José Quijada LHP
Born: 11/09/95 Age: 25 Bats: L Throws: L
Height: 5'11" Weight: 215 Origin: International Free Agent, 2013

YEAR	TEAM	LVL	AGE	W	L	SV	G	GS	IP	H	HR	BB/9	K/9	K	GB%	BABIP
2018	JAX	AA	22	0	2	4	17	0	22^1	13	1	2.8	11.7	29	31.2%	.255
2018	NO	AAA	22	2	4	3	27	0	40^2	24	2	4.9	11.5	52	32.3%	.250
2019	NO	AAA	23	1	0	4	22	0	29^1	27	5	3.7	10.7	35	33.8%	.293
2019	MIA	MLB	23	2	3	1	34	0	29^2	27	10	7.9	13.3	44	32.9%	.288
2020	LAA	MLB	24	0	1	0	6	0	3^2	6	1	4.9	14.7	6	36.4%	.500
2021 FS	LAA	MLB	25	2	2	0	57	0	50	42	8	4.7	10.7	59	34.2%	.283
2021 DC	LAA	MLB	25	2	2	0	46	0	40	34	6	4.7	10.7	47	34.2%	.283

Comparables: Tanner Scott, Richard Lovelady, Jake Newberry

Picked up on waivers in February, Quijada managed to spend the entire season on the 40-man while only pitching 3⅓ innings, in which he looked roughly the same as in his debut season (not a compliment). The Angels clearly see something worth keeping around, but "not good enough to crack the 2020 Angels bullpen" is the headliner and the punchline, all in one.

YEAR	TEAM	LVL	AGE	WHIP	ERA	DRA-	WARP	MPH	FB%	WHF	CSP
2018	JAX	AA	22	0.90	2.42	72	0.4				
2018	NO	AAA	22	1.13	3.32	67	0.9				
2019	NO	AAA	23	1.33	4.30	83	0.6				
2019	MIA	MLB	23	1.79	5.76	104	0.1	95.6	71.7%	34.3%	
2020	LAA	MLB	24	2.18	7.36	71	0.1	94.7	68.5%	33.3%	
2021 FS	LAA	MLB	25	1.38	4.46	100	0.2	95.4	71.2%	34.1%	45.7%
2021 DC	LAA	MLB	25	1.38	4.46	100	0.2	95.4	71.2%	34.1%	45.7%

Los Angeles Angels 2021

José Quintana LHP
Born: 01/24/89   Age: 32   Bats: R   Throws: L
Height: 6'1"   Weight: 220   Origin: International Free Agent, 2006

YEAR	TEAM	LVL	AGE	W	L	SV	G	GS	IP	H	HR	BB/9	K/9	K	GB%	BABIP
2018	CHC	MLB	29	14	11	0	33	33	179²	170	27	3.5	8.3	165	42.0%	.291
2019	CHC	MLB	30	13	9	0	32	31	171	191	20	2.4	8.0	152	43.6%	.329
2020	CHC	MLB	31	0	0	0	4	1	10	10	1	2.7	10.8	12	42.3%	.360
2021 FS	LAA	MLB	32	9	8	0	26	26	150	144	23	2.5	8.6	142	43.4%	.290
2021 DC	LAA	MLB	32	9	7	0	25	25	139.7	134	22	2.5	8.6	133	43.4%	.290

Comparables: Rick Porcello, Masahiro Tanaka, Matt Harvey

Even by 2020 standards, Quintana had an abbreviated season brought about by an unfortunate dishwashing accident. After a slippery knife caused the once reliable southpaw to go under one, he returned for a nondescript 10 innings of league-average work. After nearly a decade as a steady mid-rotation arm, Quintana will likely have to settle for a back-end gig.

YEAR	TEAM	LVL	AGE	WHIP	ERA	DRA-	WARP	MPH	FB%	WHF	CSP
2018	CHC	MLB	29	1.33	4.11	110	0.8	93.3	68.3%	20.7%	
2019	CHC	MLB	30	1.39	4.68	92	2.3	92.9	61.8%	20.9%	
2020	CHC	MLB	31	1.30	4.50	92	0.1	93.5	60.1%	27.6%	
2021 FS	LAA	MLB	32	1.24	3.88	91	2.2	93.1	63.8%	21.3%	47.4%
2021 DC	LAA	MLB	32	1.24	3.88	91	1.9	93.1	63.8%	21.3%	47.4%

Chris Rodriguez RHP
Born: 07/20/98   Age: 22   Bats: R   Throws: R
Height: 6'2"   Weight: 185   Origin: Round 4, 2016 Draft (#126 overall)

YEAR	TEAM	LVL	AGE	W	L	SV	G	GS	IP	H	HR	BB/9	K/9	K	GB%	BABIP
2019	IE	HI-A	20	0	0	0	3	3	9¹	6	0	3.9	12.5	13	68.4%	.316
2021 FS	LAA	MLB	22	2	2	0	57	0	50	45	7	3.9	8.7	48	43.2%	.283

Comparables: Ian Anderson, Danny Duffy, Beau Burrows

Once again healthy after a back injury and related issues limited him to three starts at High-A ball between 2018 and 2019, the exigency that was 2020 prevented Rodriguez from getting fully back on track. He still impressed enough at the Angels' alternate site, with his upper-90s velocity, to be added to the 40-man roster for Rule 5 protection. The track to the majors, especially for pitchers, has always provided plenty of puddles to jump in the best of times.

YEAR	TEAM	LVL	AGE	WHIP	ERA	DRA-	WARP	MPH	FB%	WHF	CSP
2019	IE	HI-A	20	1.07	0.00	64	0.2				
2021 FS	LAA	MLB	22	1.35	4.25	98	0.3				

José Suarez LHP

Born: 01/03/98 Age: 23 Bats: L Throws: L
Height: 5'10" Weight: 225 Origin: International Free Agent, 2014

YEAR	TEAM	LVL	AGE	W	L	SV	G	GS	IP	H	HR	BB/9	K/9	K	GB%	BABIP
2018	IE	HI-A	20	0	1	0	2	2	9	6	0	1.0	18.0	18	66.7%	.400
2018	MOB	AA	20	2	1	0	7	7	29^2	34	0	2.4	15.5	51	36.8%	.500
2018	SL	AAA	20	1	4	0	17	17	78^1	81	5	4.0	8.4	73	47.6%	.336
2019	SL	AAA	21	2	1	0	7	6	32^1	24	3	4.7	8.6	31	44.3%	.247
2019	LAA	MLB	21	2	6	0	19	15	81	100	23	3.7	8.0	72	36.2%	.326
2020	LAA	MLB	22	0	2	0	2	2	2^1	10	1	19.3	7.7	2	46.7%	.643
2021 FS	LAA	MLB	23	8	9	0	26	26	150	153	26	4.9	8.6	143	39.8%	.302
2021 DC	LAA	MLB	23	4	2	0	27	3	42.7	43	7	4.9	8.6	40	39.8%	.302

Comparables: Kolby Allard, Jaime Barria, Luis Severino

It was easy to dismiss Suarez's rookie 2019, when circumstance pressed him into major-league service well ahead of schedule, and predictable results ensured. The follow-up campaign might be just as easy to hand-wave as a mere two starts; how much can we learn from two starts? Two gory statlines, though, compound, even before getting into the *fun fact** (*not for Angels fans) portion of this comment: Another Angels pitcher, Shohei Ohtani, made a dismal statement with two 2020 starts, and his near-40 ERA would be the fourth-worst pitcher season in Angels history (no minimum innings) if Suarez's own astounding ERA didn't edge him out. As with Ohtani, should Suarez' 2021 not provide answers, the questions will threaten to drown out all else in depressing noise.

YEAR	TEAM	LVL	AGE	WHIP	ERA	DRA-	WARP	MPH	FB%	WHF	CSP
2018	IE	HI-A	20	0.78	2.00	17	0.5				
2018	MOB	AA	20	1.42	3.03	54	0.9				
2018	SL	AAA	20	1.48	4.48	95	1.0				
2019	SL	AAA	21	1.27	3.62	53	1.3				
2019	LAA	MLB	21	1.64	7.11	184	-2.9	93.3	47.2%	25.3%	
2020	LAA	MLB	22	6.43	38.57	152	0.0	94.7	45.5%	32.4%	
2021 FS	LAA	MLB	23	1.57	5.55	118	-0.1	93.4	47.0%	25.9%	46.2%
2021 DC	LAA	MLB	23	1.57	5.55	118	-0.1	93.4	47.0%	25.9%	46.2%

Angels Prospects

The State of the System:
We aren't too sad that we don't have to figure out where exactly to rank Jo Adell now, but his graduation does take a bite out of the impact prospect group at the top.

The Top Ten:

1 ★ ★ ★ *2021 Top 101 Prospect* #44 ★ ★ ★
Brandon Marsh CF   OFP: 60   ETA: 2021
Born: 12/18/97   Age: 23   Bats: L   Throws: R   Height: 6'4"   Weight: 215
Origin: Round 2, 2016 Draft (#60 overall)

The Report: Marsh is a well-rounded outfielder who can contribute in a variety of ways. At 6-foot-4 and 215-pounds, the left-handed hitter has yet to tap into his reservoir of power, but his display of hard contact to all fields while hitting .300 at Double-A in 2019 is a great sign of his future offensive potential. His speed translates to plus range in the outfield and he has the arm strength to play all three positions. Marsh is an excellent baserunner and a capable thief, stealing 18-of-23 bases while in the Southern League. Marsh could entrench himself in the middle of a big-league lineup very soon.

Development Track: Marsh's versatility and undeniable talent could allow him to force his way into the lineup as soon as next season.

Variance: Low. Additional leverage in the swing would equate to more power, as long as it doesn't compromise the already impressive hard contact ability.

Mark Barry's Fantasy Take: OK, so the dream is for Marsh to add a little more pop to an already pretty well-rounded base of skills. And while that would certainly be very cool (as the kids say), Marsh could still be awfully valuable in a fantasy sense even without prodigious power. There are faint whiffs of an Adam Eaton-esque floor, even if Marsh only slugs 12-15 homers. An Eaton floor with plenty of upside to be better puts Marsh firmly amongst the top-30 dynasty prospects on my personal list.

Los Angeles Angels 2021

2 ★ ★ ★ *2021 Top 101 Prospect* **#76** ★ ★ ★

Jordyn Adams CF   OFP: 60   ETA: 2022
Born: 10/18/99   Age: 21   Bats: R   Throws: R   Height: 6'2"   Weight: 180
Origin: Round 1, 2018 Draft (#17 overall)

The Report: Adams is an elite defender in center field and continues to develop his dynamic offensive game. The speed, agility, and soft hands that made him a highly recruited prep wide receiver are apparent as he ranges gap-to-gap on defense. He's demonstrated advanced strike zone awareness in his two seasons thus far (.353 career OBP), and reportedly held his own while facing older pitching at the Angels' alternate site in 2020.

Development Track: While advanced pitching has been able to knock the bat out of his hands on occasion, those days are dwindling as the young outfielder develops into an offensive presence. While he may never hit more than 20-25 home runs in a season, his middle-of-the field approach and high rate of contact should equate to a perennial .270-.290 hitter.

Variance: Medium. The bat-to-ball ability requires improvement before he can solidify his spot in a lineup.

Mark Barry's Fantasy Take: Admittedly, I might be a sucker for Angels outfield prospects with the initials J.A., but I quite like Adams. Adams is never going to reach Jo Adell's power potential, but he can get on base and run, and he'll also get plenty of shots thanks to superb defense. Production-wise, might I interest you in a ceiling of Deluxe Ender Inciarte

3 ★ ★ ★ *2021 Top 101 Prospect* **#86** ★ ★ ★

Reid Detmers LHP   OFP: 55   ETA: 2022
Born: 07/08/99   Age: 21   Bats: L   Throws: L   Height: 6'2"   Weight: 210
Origin: Round 1, 2020 Draft (#10 overall)

The Report: It would be difficult to find a better performing starting pitcher at the collegiate level the past two years than Detmers. He racked up strikeouts at an eye-popping rate and displayed good control with low walk totals, so you'd expect it to be coming from an electric flame-thrower. Not the case with Detmers, whose fastball is average on pure velocity, but plays up due to his plus command of the pitch inside the strike zone. The separator in the arsenal is a big breaking curveball that locks up hitters with regularity. Hitters often attempt to protect against the curve, leaving them susceptible to swinging late on the heater. His build is solid with a strong lower half and he has mechanics that stay consistent, lending evaluators to feel confident about a starter's role, albeit with a limited ceiling.

Development Track: There is some belief the fastball has potential left if Detmers can develop more efficient back-spin and work up in the zone with the pitch to further complement the curve. Without much room left to add on his frame, the velocity is likely to remain in the low 90s, necessitating improvement in other areas to help on the overall quality of his pitches. His changeup has some feel to it with late sinking action; having been able to get through lineups in college mostly as a two-pitch pitcher, further work wouldn't hurt to make it a weak-contact option against righties.

Variance: Low. The flags and question marks are limited. With the state of the big league club's pitching staff, they could really use some consistency in the rotation.

Mark Barry's Fantasy Take: Typically I'm out on low-velocity, two-pitch hurlers like Detmers, but I'm definitely more interested when plus command is involved. The changeup will likely determine the southpaw's upside, and while we won't know about its development before most FYPDs, I'm taking a flyer on Detmers as a top-150 prospect and a potential top-10 FYPD selection.

4. Kyren Paris SS   OFP: 55   ETA: 2024
Born: 11/11/01   Age: 19   Bats: R   Throws: R   Height: 6'0"   Weight: 165
Origin: Round 2, 2019 Draft (#55 overall)

The Report: A big "arrow up" pop-up player out of southern California the spring before the 2019 draft, Paris is a promising infielder in a number of ways, perhaps most notably via the analytics. As one of the youngest players in the draft, data-driven models weigh age relative to potential since there is a presumption of more room for all-encompassing growth. Paris clearly fit that bill and is said to have been working his tail off in the weight room. Whether he stays at shortstop or moves to another position is contingent on how fully he fills out the uniform. He could also be at second or third, or even the outfield thanks to his rangy footspeed and quick reactions. The swing is simple and includes ideal actions with the hands, balanced throughout and a bat-path that stays level through the zone.

Development Track: Paris missed most of his pro debut after the draft thanks to a broken hamate bone, and then we had the lost year of 2020, meaning he's sorely needing the game reps to get his feet wet. The good news, experience notwithstanding, reports have been favorable with regards to his training makeup. With no games to play, all indicators point to making the most of the time off, now requiring a healthy 2021 to make up for lost time.

Variance: Extreme. He's young, very young when you consider how long it's been since he's played in meaningful games. Until he gets on the field for a sustained season it's impossible to know where he's at as a position player with a two-year layoff.

Mark Barry's Fantasy Take: Paris has 13 professional plate appearances, thanks to a broken hamate bone and, well, 2020. There's a chance he could be a "solid-across-the-board" contributor, but he's still very far away in terms of development, so everything is a complete guess right now for our purposes. I think I speak for us all when I say that I hope Paris is very good, if not great, for a handful of years before bowing out of the fantasy spotlight, so we can all knowingly glance at one another and earnestly say, "We'll always have Paris."

5. Chris Rodriguez   RHP   OFP: 55   ETA: 2022
Born: 07/20/98   Age: 22   Bats: R   Throws: R   Height: 6'2"   Weight: 185
Origin: Round 4, 2016 Draft (#126 overall)

The Report: Rodriguez has been severely limited by injuries, throwing just 9 ⅓ innings across the 2018-19 seasons. When healthy, the 22-year-old right-hander showcases an electric four-pitch repertoire featuring a heavy, mid-90s fastball. Accompanying the heat are two different breaking balls, a hard lateral slider and a downward-tumbling curveball, along with an effective, dawdling changeup.

Development Track: Strictly utilized as a starter up to this point in his career, Rodriguez's injury history and power repertoire make the bullpen an option. Reportedly healthy and impressive at the Angels' alternate site and instructs in 2020, Rodriguez is more than ready to resume his promising career.

Variance: High. Has to stay on the field to progress.

Mark Barry's Fantasy Take: Four-pitch mixes are wonderful. However, they're less useful if one can't stay on the field. I'll keep Rodriguez on the watchlist for now and act accordingly if/when he stays healthy for an extended period of time.

6. Jeremiah Jackson   SS   OFP: 55   ETA: 2023
Born: 03/26/00   Age: 21   Bats: R   Throws: R   Height: 6'0"   Weight: 165
Origin: Round 2, 2018 Draft (#57 overall)

The Report: We were impressed with Jackson's pop out of a presently thin but projectable frame during his 2019 Pioneer League jaunt and saw him as a potential plus power/speed shortstop. He was a long way from that projection due to an aggressive approach coupled with an unorthodox hand load that created length and left him vulnerable to better spin. The defense in the infield was shaky at times as well, although the underlying tools were enough to man the position given year-over-year development.

Development Track: Jackson got alternate site and instructional league reps, but we didn't get the kind of reports that would markedly move him one way or the other. Which, given where he was entering the season, is a bit of a net negative for the projection.

Variance: Very High. It was high last year for the hit tool and lack of full-season experience/performance. Another year older, and deeper in debt (to variance).

Mark Barry's Fantasy Take: We're currently smack dab in the middle of the Golden Age of Fantasy Shortstops, but at his peak, Jackson could sneak into the back end of the top 15 at the position, thanks to some solid pop. He's a top-150 prospect, but it's hard to imagine him scraping into the top 50.

7. D'Shawn Knowles OF

OFP: 55   **ETA:** 2023/2024
Born: 01/16/01   **Age:** 20   **Bats:** S   **Throws:** R   **Height:** 6'0"   **Weight:** 165
Origin: International Free Agent, 2017

The Report: Knowles is a fleet-of-foot, up-the-middle type with some feel to hit and above-average bat speed from both sides of the plate. The swing isn't built for much game power, but he could add some doubles and maybe even 40 over-the-fence pop if he gets stronger in his 20s—and he did show off some ability to lift the ball in last winter's Bahamian Home Run Derby (look, there hasn't been much baseball this year, so I will use what little I have). Realistically though, you are hoping for a slash-and-burn center fielder who hits it in the gaps enough to get to 40 doubles. And he still hasn't seen full-season pitching and just lost an important year of development time.

Development Track: I wrote in our Rule 5 Draft recap that one of the reasons that perhaps a better class of prospect was available this year was that teams didn't have the extra season of reps in which to evaluate if a player should be protected (or put another way, would be likely to get taken). That also applies to the BP Prospect Team as we try to evaluate a certain class of prospect. On our first list I suggested it would be primarily prospects with upside, but little or no full-season experience. Knowles is a prime example of this problem. One could argue that ranking him on the 101 last year was a year too early. We make this kind of bet on occasion, especially towards the very back of the list. The difference in evaluation and projection between the 100th-best prospect and 150th best is marginal, but one gets a line on the prospect's b-ref page and one doesn't. Knowles was very high variance coming into 2020. I believed in the hit tool. I thought he might add some power. But there was certainly a non-zero chance he would go to the Midwest League and flop. There was also a non-zero chance he would end the year in the Cal League as a borderline Top 50 prospect in baseball. Neither of those happened. He didn't stand out at instructs in particular, but in a year like this, how much do you hold that against him? We don't know anything more than we did last year. I'm not moving the line much here. But Knowles won't make the 101, and where I do have information about improvements in the system, he's been passed for now.

Variance: Extreme. Using the same basic principle as Jackson, Knowles was very high last year and only got some instructs reps in 2020.

Mark Barry's Fantasy Take: First and foremost, I'm currently petitioning BP to send me to next year's Bahamanian Home Run Derby, you know, for research.

After that, well, not much has happened in the last year for Knowles to have improved his profile. Unfortunately, Knowles needs reps to develop and the last 365 days haven't been helpful in that regard. I would have pushed for Knowles to be added to the dynasty farm system last season around this time, but currently, I think he's a watchlist guy.

Los Angeles Angels 2021

8 Jack Kochanowicz OFP: 55 ETA: 2024
Born: 12/22/00 Age: 20 Bats: L Throws: R Height: 6'6" Weight: 220
Origin: Round 3, 2019 Draft (#92 overall)

The Report: A tall, sturdy, cold weather prep arm, Kochanowicz still technically hasn't thrown a professional pitch. When he was drafted he was sitting low 90s, touching higher, along with having a projectable curve and firm change. Your standard cold weather pitching starter kit. Despite his size, the mechanics are repeatable, and he shows good body control keeping all his moving parts in line. A quick arm action and long stride makes the fastball play up and get on hitters quickly, and he stays tall to create plane on the pitch as well. It's a starter's frame and delivery. Kochanowicz just needs the three-pitch arsenal to develop.

Development Track: Despite not being a particular projectable 6-foot-6, Kochanowicz showed up to instructs sitting mid-90s rather than bumping there. That's a strong base for development, and it also creates a little more separation off his changeup. He might have headed to (checks crib sheet) Inland Empire in 2021 regardless, but the lack of short-season landing spots means he will have to try and develop his secondaries in the less-than-friendly confines of the Cal League.

Variance: Extreme. Very limited pro experience, more than the usual secondary development needed for a prep arm.

Mark Barry's Fantasy Take: The bones are there, to be sure. But the reps against anything nearing professional hitters have not been, so Kochanowicz should be on the radar in leagues with 350ish prospects, but probably not otherwise—you know, until we see him be a professional pitcher or whatever.

9 Orlando Martinez RF OFP: 50 ETA: 2022
Born: 02/17/98 Age: 23 Bats: L Throws: L Height: 6'0" Weight: 185
Origin: International Free Agent, 2017

The Report: An ideal fourth outfielder, Martinez hits for average, draws walks, runs well, plays all three outfield positions, and has enough power to pinch hit off the bench in any scenario. In 88 games in the 2019 season, Martinez totaled 12 homers and 21 doubles, alluding to the sneaky pop and offensive capabilities of the 6-foot, 180-pound lefty. He's a well-rounded ballplayer who can hit throughout the lineup, bunts, runs, provides above-average defense, and takes one for the team.

Development Track: The 22-year-old has yet to play above High-A, but is equipped with an advanced baseball IQ and the savvy skills to advance quickly to the big leagues. While his consistent but unspectacular game may not suit every lineup, his value may be greatest on a good team, where he can be utilized in favorable matchups and off of the bench.

Variance: High. While his skill set is broad, he might like a carrying tool, and he wasn't major league-ready enough to be picked in the Rule 5.

Mark Barry's Fantasy Take: I'm not sure you have to take too much action on Martinez until he a) hits for more power or 2) becomes more efficient on the bases. I don't have a ton of faith in either option, so he's probably a deep, deep or only-league play.

10. Adrian Placencia

OFP: 50 **ETA:** 2025
Born: 06/02/03 **Age:** 18 **Bats:** S **Throws:** R **Height:** 5'11" **Weight:** 155
Origin: International Free Agent, 2019

The Report: One of two seven-figure shortstops in the Angels' 2019 July 2nd class, Placencia doesn't have Arol Vera's physical projection, but his present offensive tools are advanced and he's a good enough athlete to handle short although he clearly needs more experience on the dirt because his reads off the bat reflect how few reps he's had in the grand scheme of things.

Development Track: Placencia didn't look overmatched against older and more advanced competition at domestic instructs. He has plus bat speed and a plan at the plate. The defensive tools are behind the offensive ones at present, but he's a good athlete with the hands to stay up the middle. There's some tools projection and Placencia stings the ball enough to hope he adds some power with maturity, but the overall profile is both lower ceiling and less of a lottery ticket than your median million-dollar IFA shortstop.

Variance: Extreme. The profile could go in several different directions, both generally and positionally. Placencia has been a professional baseball player for just over a year now and it's been a weird year. If you wanted to call him a 55 / Extreme right now based on holding his own against better than usual instructs competition, I wouldn't disagree strongly.

Mark Barry's Fantasy Take: Low-ceiling, not necessarily lottery ticket potential = meh on the fantasy side. The offensive skills are ahead of the defensive prowess at present, so that's something, but at present, Placencia is an assistant-to-the-watchlist as opposed to assistant watchlist.

The Prospects You Meet Outside The Top Ten

Interesting Draft Follow

Werner Blakely SS **Born:** 02/21/02 **Age:** 19 **Bats:** L **Throws:** R **Height:** 6'3" **Weight:** 185 **Origin:** Round 4, 2020 Draft (#111 overall)

One draft heuristic the Angels employ is prioritizing premium physical attributes, trusting that they can convert them into baseball skills. They went over slot in the fourth round to pry Blakely away from Auburn because of the explosive traits to his swing, which are apparent even as he's trying to find a comfortable setup. He also displays loose actions with the glove and arm, despite the question of where he will end up on the field as his 6-foot-3 body matures.

Interesting Rule 5 Draft Follow

Jose Rivera 2B   Born: 05/26/99   Age: 22   Bats: R   Throws: R   Height: 5'10"   Weight: 165   Origin: International Free Agent, 2016

José Soriano was at the back of this Top 10 list right up until the 2020 Rule 5 draft started. I'm loathe to write up Rule 5 eligible players for these lists for just that reason, but both he and Martinez were too good to leave off entirely. You could make a case to slot Rivera right in Soriano's old spot at 9 or 10. It's a broadly similar profile as I noted in our draft recap. Unlike Soriano, Rivera isn't recovering from Tommy John surgery, which isn't necessarily a positive when you have to roster him all season. His command is behind Soriano's, which is the main reason he's also outside the Top Ten and also less likely to stick on the Angels 26-(or however many) man for all of 2021. If they do manage to keep him around, they will be getting a potential fourth starter out of the deal with three 50 to 55 offerings. But either way he will still be in the Angels chapter when the Futures Guide publishes.

MLB arms, but probably relievers

Hector Yan LHP   Born: 04/26/99   Age: 22   Bats: L   Throws: L   Height: 5'11"   Weight: 180   Origin: International Free Agent, 2015

Yan's fastball can touch the upper 90s and his slider can flash plus. The split is good enough he won't need to drop it in relief, but relief is where he's going to end up given the control issues emanating from his unorthodox delivery. He'll need to smooth that all out even in one-inning stints, though, to be more than a Jekyll-or-Hyde extra 'pen arm.

MLB bats, but less upside than you'd like

Jahmai Jones 2B   Born: 08/04/97   Age: 23   Bats: R   Throws: R   Height: 6'0"   Weight: 204   Origin: Round 2, 2015 Draft (#70 overall)

The former Top 101 prospect—two years and one position switch ago—finally made the majors in 2020. The game power never consistently showed up outside of the Cal League, and Jones struggled more generally in Double-A. He's significantly changed his swing in recent seasons, and now is very quiet with just a toe tap and an exaggerated hand position that simplifies his route to the pitch. The profile is still a little short for a starting second baseman, but if you add an outfield glove back to his locker, Jones could be a useful bench piece.

Top Talents 25 and Under (as of 4/1/2021):

1. Jo Adell, OF
2. Brandon Marsh, OF
3. Griffin Canning, RHP

4. Jordyn Adams, OF
5. Reid Detmers, LHP
6. Kyren Paris, SS
7. Chris Rodriguez, RHP
8. Jeremiah Jackson, SS
9. D'Shawn Knowles, OF
10. Patrick Sandoval, LHP

Jo Adell, our No. 2 prospect in baseball the past two seasons, (barely) graduated from rookie-eligibility with the modified service time rules. He still ranks first here quite comfortably, but that saved us from some difficult discussions about how much to shade down his hit tool projection based on how bad he looked in the majors in 2020. Adell missed in the zone so much that I had a semi-serious conversation with Craig Goldstein right towards the end of the season about whether he might be having trouble seeing the ball, a la Wilson Ramos. It was only 132 plate appearances at 21-years-old in a pandemic season, so we're not exactly alarmed, but making contact on less than 65 percent of pitches in the strike zone is cause for at least moderate concern.

Griffin Canning is the rare third starter prospect who seems to be settling in as exactly a third starter. He's had somewhat chronic elbow injuries dating back to college, and probably wouldn't have been ready if the 2020 season had started on time with UCL injuries. But he avoided surgery, and was fine by summer camp. Ultimately, he made 11 league-average starts. We're shading Canning behind Marsh this year given the lack of superior upside and the shaky medical history, but he's likely to keep trucking as a mid-rotation pitcher as long as he's healthy.

Patrick Sandoval is a lefty with a feel for spin and velocity who has been ridiculously homer-prone in the majors but could yet round out into a decent major-league starter. Jaime Barria had his first above-replacement season in 2020 by DRA, with 32 $\frac{1}{3}$ semi-effective innings; he's got a usable fastball/slider combination but could use to miss more bats if he's going to be more than a bulk innings type. Luis Rengifo was a long-time favorite of our late colleague and friend Rob McQuown; he's failed to hit for average much in part-time play in two MLB seasons even though he was a hit-tool oriented prospect. Matt Thaiss is a walks-first first baseman who has started picking up other positions; he'd be even more interesting if he picked back up the catching mitt he left at the University of Virginia. José Suarez barely made the back of this list last year, before he made two starts that lasted 2 $\frac{1}{3}$ innings combined.

Part 3: Featured Articles

Angels All-Time Top 10 Players

by Matthew Trueblood

POSITION PLAYERS

DARIN ERSTAD, 1B/OF (1996-2006)
In baseball history, only four players have spent at least 20 percent of their careers at each of Erstad's three main defensive positions: first base, center field, and left field. The other three are Felipe Alou, Al Oliver, and Brad Wilkerson. With those players, their positional progress was a simple slide down the defensive spectrum and a reflection of their teams' desire to get their bats in the lineup. With Erstad, it was the opposite. He was only a usable hitter (career DRC+: 91, with that magical 2000 season propping it up even that high), but was a brilliant fielder at all three spots. His only weakness was a poor arm. On Angels teams that had to cover for Tim Salmon, Garret Anderson, Mo Vaughn, Vladimir Guerrero, and other plodding defenders, his versatility and excellence were vital.

BOBBY GRICH, 2B (1977-1986)
Sixteen years into their existence, the Angels had had four winning seasons and had never finished higher than third place in their league or division. The advent of free agency gave them a chance to change that, and Grich (one of the most sought-after stars of the first full-fledged class) helped them turn the corner. An early sabermetric darling, he hit for low batting averages but had above-average power for a second baseman (with the friendly left-field dimensions at Angel Stadium, above-average power, period), got on base at a high clip thanks to good plate discipline, and played good defense. He brought an edge, too. In his decade with the club, they had five winning seasons, and made the ALCS three times. The worst thing you can say about him is he tried to lift an air-conditioner prior to the 1977 season with predictable results.

HOWIE KENDRICK, 2B (2006-2014)

Somehow, Kendrick was just a 10th-round pick out of a Florida community college. He immediately proved that the baseball world had missed by letting him slide so far by hitting over .360 in over 1,500 plate appearances on his way up the chain. He earned top prospect status before finally reaching the big leagues, and though he didn't quite reproduce those batting averages, he more or less came as advertised. Few 21st-century hitters have been as relentlessly good at going the opposite way, particularly with ground balls and line drives. Kendrick hit .292 and was a tough out for almost a decade in Anaheim.

JIM FREGOSI, SS (1961-1971)

The moral arc of the Fregosiverse does not bend toward justice, it only bends toward oblivion in the form of having everything about Jim except his being traded for Nolan Ryan be forgotten. That's violently unfair. Fregosi did everything well, save avoid strikeouts. He was a plus-plus defender at shortstop for most of his 20s. From 1963 through 1967, he was worth at least 3.5 WARP every year. Only true legends age well at shortstop, though. The Angels traded Fregosi at just the right time—for everyone but him.

ERICK AYBAR, SS (2006-2015)

Aybar had very little pop but plenty of speed and a good enough feel to hit to muster a solid number of doubles each year. He put pressure on defenses with his speed, consistently adding half a win of value with his legs alone. It took him a while to force his way into the everyday shortstop job, but once he did, he spent a few seasons as one of the best defenders in baseball. It's easy to forget that bit, however, since the Angels eventually traded him (and two other players) for Andrelton Simmons.

BRIAN DOWNING, OF/DH/C (1978-1990)

A pitcher in high school, Downing was too small to stay on the mound as a professional. He drifted through various positions during his ascent through the White Sox system, eventually establishing himself as a catcher. He stayed there for his first seven-plus big-league seasons, but then a funny sequence took place. After requiring elbow surgery, he spent his rehab lifting weights maniacally, and came out of it with a Randy Arozarena-ic physique. The following season, he posted a 137 DRC+, far above his previous norms. Between the diminished arm strength, the new body, and the sudden power surge, another position change was in order, so he spent his 30s as a relentless, slugging left fielder and DH. From 1982-88, for mostly good Angels teams, he averaged 23 home runs and 82 walks per year. He was an excellent leadoff hitter despite being no threat to steal—it's on-base percentage that matters, not speed, and Downing's was .372.

TIM SALMON, OF (1992-2006)

"Mr. Angel" came up as the team was tumbling down into a period of significant frustration and turnover. Salmon provided stability throughout those years, stuck with the club, and was rewarded at the end of his career with a few glorious seasons of success, including a World Series ring. Seemingly reinventing his stance and tweaking his approach every few years, he found ways to produce very consistently, with a swing that reliably produced plenty of long fly balls to left field and the plate discipline to get on base often.

GARRET ANDERSON, OF (1994-2008)

Before most teams (let alone fans) fully understood where runs come from, Anderson was highly respected—even overrated. He was never a good defender, though he spent surprisingly little time as a designated hitter. He hit for truly excellent power for only a few years, and even then, he walked too infrequently to be an elite batter. With a short, simple swing, though, he made tons of contact and tended to hit line drives and find gaps with regularity. Setting up with his front foot pointing toward the pitcher's mound made that quick whip of the wood easy, and Anderson sustained roughly average production through his mid-30s.

MIKE TROUT, OF (2011-PRESENT)

Every statistical superlative we could stack at Trout's feet is already familiar to you. The numbers live up to their name, dulling the sense of awe we ought to feel at the power and grace of Trout. Instead of further studying them, then, take a moment to meditate on his swing. A decade on, he's undergone incremental changes as the league desperately assails whatever small flaw it finds, and he relentlessly covers it. In its present form, Trout's swing starts with a thunderous leg kick, generating much of his power; it flows into that lightning-quick, almost alligator-armed flash of the hands. He closes with the immaculate meetup of barrel and ball, then the short, fully controlled, two-handed finish. His trademark contact, the ball arcing out on a hard line toward left field, is equal parts gorgeous and terrible, as all natural wonders are.

CHONE FIGGINS, UTIL (2002-2009)

Establishing himself just as Erstad was fading, Figgins became his replacement as Mike Scioscia's Swiss Army knife. Even faster than Erstad and always willing to take a walk, Figgins also threw right-handed, allowing him to play more infield than Erstad could. This he did, and did well, but he was almost at the end of his Angels tenure before he settled in at any one position. He's remembered especially for making his walk year his walk year, drawing 101 free passes and baiting the Mariners into a disappointing contract, but he was worth at least 2.0 WARP in all six of his full seasons with Los Angeles.

Los Angeles Angels 2021

PITCHERS

DEAN CHANCE, RHP (1961-1966)

There was a whiff of right-handed Chris Sale to Chance, whom the Angels got in a trade just after the 1960 expansion draft. He established himself as a valuable swingman by age 21. In 1962 and in 1964 he cruised to the Cy Young Award. That season he led American League starters in innings, wins, ERA, FIP, and WARP. His peak was short, largely because of a twisting, rangy, crossfire delivery (with a Salesque arm angle). While he was at it, though, he slung one of the league's sneakiest fastballs, a tough slider, and a changeup with uncommon movement. He'd tease lefties by nibbling at the outside corner, and abuse righties by mixing his sinker and slider.

NOLAN RYAN, RHP (1972-1979)

Ryan pitched more innings for the Angels than for any other team. In his eight seasons in Anaheim he led the American League in strikeouts seven times and in hits allowed per nine innings five times (although also in walks six times, and in wild pitches three times). His strikeout rate was more than double that of the average pitcher during his Angels tenure. He struck batters out at a higher rate (relative to his peers) than Craig Kimbrel, Aroldis Chapman, or Billy Wagner have during their careers, while pitching more innings in those eight years than the three of them have so far combined to pitch over their careers.

FRANK TANANA, LHP (1973-1980)

By any modern standard, Tanana was a victim of severe pitcher abuse. In his age-20 season of 1974, he faced 1,127 batters. From that season through 1978, he faced at least 973 batters every year, and pitched 81 complete games. From 1975 through the first half of 1978, he was one of the game's elite hurlers, with a fastball and power curve no one could touch. Then, predictably, he broke. He sputtered to the finish in 1978, with a 5.22 ERA and cratering strikeout rate over the final two months. He missed half of 1979 and was never the same. The Angels shipped him to Boston in the Fred Lynn trade, and he hung on for another dozen years as a league-average junkballer.

MIKE WITT, RHP (1981-1990)

The Angels of the 1970s and 1980s allowed hurlers with tremendous promise to pitch way too much at young ages, stunting their development and shortening their careers in the name of maximizing short-term workloads. Witt, a local kid taken in the fourth round, made good almost immediately, pitching 129 strong innings at age 20, in the strike-shortened season of 1981. A scrawny 6-foot-7, Witt used an overhand delivery that made his curveball devastating, his fastball intimidating, and (because of how often he was asked to throw that way) his arm practically useless by age 30. By then, the Angels had gotten a handful of good, workhorse seasons from him, and they were able to swap him for the ageless Dave Winfield before he turned into a pumpkin. His end-of-season perfect game against the Rangers on September 30, 1984 remains a franchise highlight.

CHUCK FINLEY, LHP (1986-1999)

Vastly underrated, Finley hovered between good and great for most of a decade and a half. He was a tall, imposing southpaw, and threw from a high three-quarters slot that accentuated his size. He didn't depend on power, throwing a four-seamer, sinker, and cutter, plus a split-change that flummoxed righties; a slurvy slider for lefties; and a slow curve that he could use to maximize contrast against anyone. He was worth at least 4.3 WARP in six different seasons for the Angels.

MARK LANGSTON, LHP (1990-1997)

Langston had great stuff which he used to rack up strikeouts in the first phase of his career, but shaky control held him back for much of that time. By the time he hit free agency after 1989, he was a bit less overpowering, but had begun to find the plate with much greater consistency. The Angels got somewhat uneven work from him, but he racked up big innings totals for them, made three All-Star teams, and won five Gold Glove awards in a row. His slider, curveball and changeup had all become useful complements to his heat by the time he settled in for the Angels.

TROY PERCIVAL, RHP (1995-2004)

Before there was Kenley Jansen, there was Percival, whom the Angels drafted as a little-known catching prospect in 1990. His arm was so impressive that he made a quick transition to the mound but he still didn't reach the big leagues until 1995. Once he did, it was lights-out thanks to a fastball that sat just under 100 miles per hour and sometimes touched that number. In his early 30s, he developed a degenerative hip condition, sapping much of that velocity, but he racked up 316 saves for the Angels—plus seven in the 2002 postseason, still tied for the most in any single October, including the final out of Game 7 of the World Series.

JARROD WASHBURN, LHP (1998-2005)

In our DRA database, which goes back to 1950, only two pitchers have thrown as many career innings as Washburn (over 1,800) and had an ERA that beat their DRA by a wider margin. Washburn was viewed as an enigma: There was nothing he did especially well, yet he consistently posted average or better ERAs. He threw a fairly straight fastball. He lacked overpowering velocity. He rarely used his secondary stuff and didn't miss bats with it. Yet, in over 1,100 innings with the Angels, he prevented runs 13 percent better than an average hurler.

Los Angeles Angels 2021

JOHN LACKEY, RHP (2002-2009)

Game 7 of the 2002 World Series found the Angels in need of a good showing under maximum pressure, from a fresh-faced rookie. Lackey gave it to them. He seemed to reach the majors fully formed with a hulking frame, four good pitches, and a fearless intensity that would become his trademark. He proudly pitched deep into games and bore heavy overall workloads. From 2005-07, he was worth 18.1 WARP.

JERED WEAVER, RHP (2006-2016)

During his peak, Weaver was an absolute joy to watch. Big and stringy with a surfer's haircut and chin beard, he would start on the third-base side of the pitching rubber, stride even further that direction, but then tilt his spine, vault toward the plate, and fire from an over-the-top angle. Hitters saw crossfire action like that of a sidearmer, but Weaver's four-seamer had more rising action than all but two other starters in the PITCHf/x Era. If anyone got comfortable with that pitch, he then wrecked them with a snapdragon slider. Before a rapid and early decline, he piled up 1,700 innings with an ERA of 3.27.

A Taxonomy of 2020 Abnormalities

by Rob Mains

I'm going to start this with a trivia question. Trust me, it's relevant. Don't bother skipping to the end of the article to find the answer, it's not there.

Only five players have appeared in 140 or more games for 16 straight seasons. Who are they?

It's a trivia question starting off an essay, so you know how this works: Whatever you guessed, you're wrong. It's okay. As someone who purchased this book, chances are good that you're an educated baseball fan. But the circumstances behind 2020 force us to abandon, or at least seriously question, some of our favorite patterns and crutches for evaluating the game we love.

We just completed what was undoubtedly the strangest season in MLB history. No fans, geographically limited schedule, universal DH, seven-inning twin bills, runners on second in extra innings, a 16-team postseason, a club playing at a Triple-A stadium. Some of these changes will likely persist (sorry), but we've never had so many tweaks dumped on us all at once, at least not since they figured out how many balls were in a walk.

And the biggest, of course, was the 60-game season. The 19th century was dotted with teams that went bankrupt before the season ended, but the lone season with only 60 scheduled games was 1877. That year there were only six teams, the league rostered a total of 77 players (just 16 more than the 2020 Marlins), and batters called for pitches to be thrown high or low by the pitcher, who was 50 feet away. We can say the 2020 season was easily the shortest ever for recognizable baseball.

As such, it'll stand out. Few abbreviated seasons do. Just about everybody reading this knows the 1994 season ended after Seattle's Randy Johnson struck out Oakland's Ernie Young for the last out of the Mariners-A's game on August 11. The ensuing player strike wiped out the rest of the season and the postseason. Teams played only 112-117 games that year.

And many of you know that a strike in the middle of the 1981 season split the season in two, resulting in the only Division Series until 1995. Teams played only 103-111 games that year, the shortest regular season since 1885.

Those two seasons are memorable. So when we see that nobody drove in 100 runs in 1981, or that Greg Maddux was the only pitcher with 180 or more innings pitched in 1994, we think, "Of course. Strike year."

But we don't remember other short years. You might not recall that the 1994 strike spilled into the next year, chopping 18 games off the 1995 schedule. You might've read that the 1918 season, played during the last pandemic, ended after Labor Day due to the government's World War I "work or fight" order. A strike erased the first week and a half of the 1972 season, but that year's best known as the last time pitchers batted in the American League.

The point is, while we don't remember small changes to the schedule, we remember the big ones. The 1981 mid-season strike. The 1994 season- and Series-ending strike. And, of course, the pandemic-shortened 2020 season. We won't need a reminder why Marcell Ozuna's 18 homers were the fewest to lead the National League in a century. (Literally; Cy Williams led with 15 in 1920.)

Now, about that trivia question. The five players are Hank Aaron, Brooks Robinson, Pete Rose, Ichiro Suzuki, and Johnny Damon. The one nobody gets, of course, is Damon, and a lot of people miss Ichiro, whose last season of 140-plus games came garbed in the red-orange and ocean blue of Miami when he was 42. That's half of what makes it a good question. The other half is the two guys whom many think made the list but didn't. Lou Gehrig? His streak started in the Yankees' 42nd game of the 1925 season and lasted only 13 seasons after that. And everybody assumes Cal Ripken Jr. did it, having played 2,632 straight games over 17 seasons. But one of those 17 seasons was 1994, when the Orioles played only 112 games.

My point? *I just told you* everybody remembers the 1994 strike year, but everybody forgets it fell in the middle of Ripken's streak, separating the first twelve years from the last four. Just because we recall something doesn't mean it's always at the front of our minds.

Nobody is going to forget 2020, and baseball is obviously not the main reason. But there will come a time in the future when you're looking at a player's or a team's record, and there will be baffling numbers there for 2020, and you'll think, "I wonder what happened." (Not to mention the missing line for minor league players.) Just like you forgot that the 1994 strike limited Ripken to 112 games.

Try not to forget it, though. The 2020 season resulted in weird statistical results for several reasons.

There were only 60 games.
I know, duh. But that had impacts beyond counting stats like Ozuna's home run total or Yu Darvish and Shane Bieber leading the majors with eight wins. (I know, pitcher wins, but still.)

The 162-game season is the longest among major North American sports, and that duration gives us a gift. Over the course of a long season, small variations tend to even out. A player who has a ten-game hot streak will probably have a ten-game cold streak. A team that starts the year losing a bunch of close games will probably win a bunch of them. We get regression to the mean. Statistics stabilize.

Consider flipping a coin. Over the long run, we expect it to come up heads about half the time. But the fewer flips, the more variation there'll be. If you flip a coin six times, probability theory tells us you'll get at least two-third heads about 34 percent of the time. Flip it 30 times, your chance of two-thirds heads drops to five percent.

Or, relevant to this case, if you flip a coin 60 times, your chance of getting at least 36 heads—that's 60 percent—is 7.75 percent. Expand the coin-flipping to 162 times, and the chance of getting 60 percent heads drops to 0.73 percent.

In other words, the odds of an outcome that's 20 percent better (or worse) than expected is *more than ten times higher* when you flip your coin 60 times than when you do it 162 times. Call it small sample size, call lack of mean reversion, or call it luck not evening out, 162 is a lot more predictive than 60. You get much more variation over 60 games than over 162. Bieber's 1.63 ERA and 0.87 FIP aren't something we'd see over a full season, and neither is Javier Baéz's .203/.238/.360.

Some players' lines in 2020 look normal. Brian Anderson had an .811 OPS in 2019 and an .810 OPS in 2020. (He probably would have gotten that last point if he'd been given enough time.) But there are many like Bieber and Baéz, some of them from young players still establishing their talent levels. The answer to the question, "What went right or wrong for that guy in 2020?" is most likely "Nothing, it was just a 2020 thing."

Preseason training was abbreviated for hitters.
Every year, spring training drags. Players get tired of it, fans get tired of it, and you sure can tell sportswriters get tired of it. Yes, something to get everyone into shape is necessary, but does it really have to drag on for over a month? Can't we shorten it?

The 2020 season answered in the negative, at least for hitters. Warren Spahn is credited with saying that hitting is timing and pitching is upsetting timing. It appears nobody had his timing down after the abbreviated July summer camp. Through August 9—18 games into the season—MLB batters were hitting .230/.311/.395 with a .275 BABIP. That BABIP, had it held, would have been the lowest since 1968, the Year of the Pitcher. In recent years it's hovered around .300.

It didn't hold. Play returned to more normal levels the rest of the year: .249/.325/.425 with a .297 BABIP starting August 10. But batters whose play concentrated in those first two weeks wound up with ugly lines. Andrew

Benintendi went on the injured list with a season-ending rib cage strain on August 11. His final line: .103/.314/.128 in 14 games. Franchy Cordero went on the IL with a hamate bone fracture on August 9 and a .154/.185/.231 line. Even though he came back strong in a late September return, it was too late to repair his full-season numbers.

Preseason training was abbreviated for pitchers.

Every year, spring training drags. Players get tired of it, fans get tired of it ... wait, I already said that. But the abbreviated preseason was tough on pitchers, too. As noted, they had the upper hand coming out of the gate. But then they lost that hand. And then their arms, too.

The 2020 season was spread over 67 days. During those 67 days, 237 pitchers hit the Injured List, compared to 135 in the first 67 days of 2019. A lot of those IL stints, though, were COVID-19-related. Still, over the first 67 days of the 2019 season, there were 72 pitchers on the IL with arm injuries. That figure jumped to 110 in 2020, a 53 percent increase.

There are a number of factors contributing to pitcher arm injuries, ranging from usage to velocity, but it appears that attenuated preseason training played a role. A lot of pitchers had super-short seasons due to arm woes. Corey Kluber, Roberto Osuna, and Shohei Ohtani combined for seven innings, none after August 8. All suffered arm injuries. We'll never know whether they'd have fared better with a longer preseason, but we can guess how they probably feel.

Everybody played.

Rosters were set to expand from 25 to 26 in 2020, so even if we'd had a normal season, we'd have likely seen 2019's record of 1,410 players on MLB rosters broken. But due to the pandemic, rosters started the year at 30 and were cut to only 28. Add multiple COVID-19 absences and the revolving door caused by poor starts by hitters and a rash of pitcher arm injuries, and 1,289 players appeared in MLB games in 2020. The comparable figure over the first 67 days of the 2019 season was 1,109. That 16 percent increase works out to an average of six more players per team in 2020 compared to a similar slice of 2019. A future look back at 2020 rosters will include a lot of unfamiliar names.

Plus became a minus.

In advanced metrics, we adjust batter and pitcher performance for park and league/era variations. A plus sign appended to the end of a measure means that it's adjusted for park and league. It's scaled to an average of 100, with higher figures above average and lower figures below average. (Similarly, a metric with a minus is also park- and league-adjusted and scaled to 100, with lower values better.) Here at BP, our advanced measure of offensive performance is DRC+. Baseball-Reference has OPS+ and FanGraphs has wRC+.

Using park and league adjustments, we can compare Dante Bichette's 1995 Steroid Era season at pre-humidor Coors Field (.340/.364/.620, 40 homers, 128 RBI, MVP runner-up) with Jim Wynn's 1968 Year of the Pitcher season at the cavernous Astrodome (.269/.376/.474, 26 homers, 67 RBI, no MVP votes). It's not close. DRC+, OPS+, and wRC+ all give the nod to Wynn, handily. This is a useful tool. As my Baseball Prospectus colleague Patrick Dubuque tweeted last fall, "Please note that when I ask how you are, I am already adjusting for era."

The 2020 season messes up plus (and minus) stats for two reasons. First, the park adjustment was based on only 30 home games instead of the usual 81. Everything noted above regarding the short season applies, literally doubly, to park effect calculations. DRC+ uses a single-season park factor. OPS+ uses a three-year average and wRC+ five years. The figure for 2020 is suspect.

Second, OPS+ and wRC+ adjust for league: American and National. (DRC+ adjusts for opponent, regardless of league.) While there were two leagues in 2020, they were an artificial construct. To reduce travel, teams played opponents geographically, not based on league. There weren't two leagues, American and National. There were three, Western, Central, and Eastern.

That makes a difference because teams in the same league played in different run-scoring environments. AL teams scored 4.58 runs per game, NL teams 4.71. That's a small difference. But teams in the East scored 0.21 more runs per game (4.95) than teams in the West (4.74), and they both scored a lot more than Central teams (4.25). Adjusting for league misses that difference, so this book will be safe in that regard, but other sources may be distorted somewhat.

Not every game was a "game."
In 2020, the rising tide of strikeouts was finally stemmed. Strikeouts per team per game fell from 8.8 in 2019 to 8.7 in 2020. That marked the first decline after 14 straight annual increases.

In 2020, the rising tide of strikeouts rose higher. Batters struck out in 23.4 percent of plate appearances compared to 23.0 percent in 2019. That marked the 15th straight annual increase.

Both are true statements.

Because of two rule changes—seven-inning doubleheaders and runners on second in extra innings—games in 2020 were unprecedented in their brevity. There were 37.0 plate appearances per game in 2020. The only years with fewer were 1904 and 1906-1909. The average game in 2020 entailed 8.61 innings pitched, the fewest since 1899.

So when you see any per-game stats for 2020, you need to increase them by 3 or 4 percent to get them on equal footing with recent years.

Los Angeles Angels 2021

Or, better, just ignore them. Last year happened. There were major league games contested between major league teams. But when you're looking at those physical or electronic baseball cards, when you're weaving narratives over why this young player's inevitable rise to stardom fell apart or why that old veteran rekindled his magic, don't linger on the 2020 line. It was just too weird.

Thanks to Lucas Apostoleris for research assistance.

—*Rob Mains is an author of Baseball Prospectus.*

Tranches of WAR

by Russell A. Carleton

We ask "replacement level" to be a lot of things. Sometimes contradictory things. Sometimes I wonder if we know what it even means anymore. The original idea was that it represented the level of production that a team could expect to get from "freely available talent", including bench players, minor leaguers, and waiver wire pickups. It created a common benchmark to compare everyone to, and for that reason, it represented an advancement well beyond what was available at the time. In fact, it created a language and a framework for evaluating players that was not just better but *entirely* different than what came before it.

But then we started mumbling in that language. The idea behind "wins above replacement" was one part sci-fi episode and one part mathematical exercise. Imagine that a player had disappeared before the season and suddenly, in an alternate timeline, his team would have had to replace him. The distance between him and that replacement line was his value. We need to talk about that alternate timeline.

Without getting too into 2:00 am "deep conversations" with extensive navel-gazing, it's worth thinking about why one player might not be playing, while another might.

- A player might not be playing because he has a short-term injury or his manager believes that he needs a day off.
- A player might not be playing because he has a longer-term injury that requires him to be on the injured list.

There's a difference here between these two situations. In particular, the first one generally *doesn't* involve a compensatory roster move, while the second one does. It's possible, though not guaranteed, that the person who will be replacing the injured/resting player would be the same in either case. That matters. Teams generally carry a spare part for all eight position players on the diamond, although in the era of a four-player bench, those spare parts usually are the backup plan for more than one spot.

Los Angeles Angels 2021

A couple of years ago, I posed a hypothetical question. Suppose that a team had two players in its system fighting for a fourth outfielder spot. One of them was a league average hitter, but would be worth 20 runs below average if allowed to play center field for a full season. One of them was a perfectly average fielder, but would be 15 runs below average as a hitter, if allowed to play an entire season. Which of the two should the team roster? It's tempting to say the second one, as overall, he is the better player. That misses the point. A league average hitter on the bench isn't just a potential replacement for an injured outfielder. He might also pinch hit for the light-hitting shortstop in a key spot. You keep the average hitter on the roster, even though he isn't a hand-in-glove fit for one specific place on the field, because being a bench player is a different job description than being a long-term fill-in for someone. If you find yourself in need of a longer-term fill-in, you can bring the other guy up from AAA.

When we're determining the value of an everyday player though, if he had disappeared before the season and a team would have had to replace his production, they likely would have done it with a player who was a long-term fill-in type because they would have had to replace a guy who played everyday. Maybe that's the same guy that they would have rostered on their bench anyway, but we don't know. It gets to the query of what we hope to accomplish with WAR. Are we looking for an accurate modeling of reality or are we looking for a common baseline to compare everyone to? Both have their uses, but they are somewhat different questions.

Let's talk about another dichotomy.

- A player might not be playing because he isn't very good and is a bench-level player.
- A player might not be playing because there is another player on the team who has a situational advantage that makes him the better choice today. The classic case of this is a handedness platoon. On another day, he might be a better choice.

When we think about player usage, I think we're still stuck in the model that there are starters and there are scrubs. We have plenty of words for bench players or reserves or backups or utility guys. We do still have the word "platoon" in our collective vocabulary, but in the age of short benches, it's hard to construct one. It's always been hard to construct them. You have to find two players who hit with different hands, have skill sets that complement each other, and probably play the same position. In the era of the short bench, one of them had probably better double as a utility player in some way. Baseball has a two-tiered language geared toward the idea of regulars and reserves. The fact that it was so easy for me to find plenty of synonyms for "a player whose primary function is to come into a game to replace a regular player if he is injured or resting" should tell you something.

I'm always one to look for "unspoken words" in baseball. What is it called when someone is both half of a platoon and the utility infielder? That guy exists sometimes, but he reveals himself in that role—usually by accident. We don't have a word for that, and whenever I find myself saying "we don't have a word for that", I look for new opportunities. What do you call it, further, when the job of being the utility infielder is decentralized across the whole infield with occasional contributions from the left fielder? It's not even a "super-utility" player. What happens when you build your entire roster around the idea that everyone will be expected to be a triple major?

⚾ ⚾ ⚾

I think someone else beat me to this one, and on a grand scale. Platoons work because we know that hitters of the opposite hand to the pitcher get better results than hitters of the same hand, usually to the tune of about 20 points of OBP. If you want to express that in runs, it usually comes out to somewhere around 10 to 12 runs of linear weights value prorated across 650 PA. But hang on a second, now let's say that we have two players who might start today, both of roughly equal merit with the bat. One has a handedness advantage, but is the worse fielder of the two. In that case, as long as his "over the course of a season" projection as a fielder at whatever position you want to slot him into is less than a 10-run drop from the guy he might replace, then he's a better option today.

We're not used to thinking of utility players as bat-first options, who would play below-average defense at three different infield positions. That guy might hook on as a 2B/3B/LF type (Howie Kendrick, come on down!) but teams usually think to themselves that they need as their utility infielder someone who "can handle" shortstop, the toughest of the infield spots to play. If someone can do that *and* hit well, he's probably already starting somewhere, so he's not available as a utility infielder. It's easier for those glove guys to find a job. In a world where the replacement for a shortstop *has to be* the designated utility infielder, that makes sense.

But as we talked about last week, we're living in a different world. The rate at which a replacement for a regular starter turns out to be *another starter* shifting over to cover has gone way up over the last five years. There was always some of it in the game, but this has been a supernova of switcheroos. Now if your second baseman is capable of playing a decent shortstop, that 2B/3B/LF guy can swap in. He's not actually playing shortstop, and maybe the defense suffers from the switch, but if he's got enough of a bat, he might outhit those extra fielding miscues. And in doing so, he is effectively your backup shortstop.

Somewhere along the lines, teams got hip to the idea of multi-positional play from their regulars. I've written before about how you can't just put a player, however athletic, into a new position and expect much at first. The data tell us that. Eventually, players can learn to be multi-positionalists, but it takes time, roughly on the order of two months, before they're OK. But there's a hidden message in there. If you give a player some reps at a new spot, he's a reasonably gifted athlete and somewhat smart and willing to learn, he could probably pick it up enough to get to "good enough," and it doesn't take forever. You just have to be purposeful about it. Maybe you get to the point where you can start to say "he's still below average but we could move him there and get another bat into the lineup, and it's a net win."

Teams have started to build those extra lessons into their player development program. It used to be seen as a mark of weakness to be relegated to "utility player" because that meant that you were a bench player (all those synonyms above come with a side of stigma). Now, it's a way of building a team. If you get a few reps in the minors (where it doesn't count) at a spot, you'll have at least played the spot at game speed before. There are limits to how far you can push that. A slow-footed "he's out in left field because we don't have the DH" guy is never going to play short, but maybe your third baseman can try second base and not look like a total moose out there.

⚾ ⚾ ⚾

Back to WAR. I'd argue that the world of starters and scrubs is slowly disintegrating, for good cause. In the event that a regular starter really does go down with an injury–ostensibly, the alternate universe scenario that WAR is attempting to model–it makes the team a little more resilient to replacing him. And the good news is that you're more likely to be able to replace him with the best of the bench bunch, rather than the third-best guy, because the best guy doesn't have to be an exact positional match for the guy who got hurt. And that's what the manager would want to do. He'd want to replace that long-term production, not with an amalgam of everyone else who played that position, but with the best guy available from his reserves.

Now this is still WAR. We still want to retain the principle that we should be measuring a player, and not his teammates. We need some sort of common baseline, and despite what I just said, we'll still need some sort of amalgam. To construct that, I give to you the idea of the tranche. The word, if you've not heard it before, refers to a piece of a whole that is somehow segmented off. It's often used in finance to talk about layers of a financial instrument.

Here, I want you to consider that there are 30 starters at each of the seven non-battery positions (catchers should have their own WAR, since only a catcher can replace a catcher). We can identify them by playing time, and we can futz around with the definition a little bit if we need to. Next, among those who aren't in that starting pool, we identify the top tranche of the 30 best bench players, which I would again identify by playing time, and then the second and third and fourth and so on. If a player were to disappear, his manager would probably want to take a guy from that top tranche of the bench to replace him. In a world where even the starters can slide around the field, that becomes more feasible.

We can take a look at that top tranche and say "How many of them showed that they are able to play (first, second, etc.)?" and therefore could have directly substituted for the starter? How many of them could have been a direct substitute for our injured player? We don't know whether one of them would be on *a specific* team, but we can say that 40 percent of the time, a manager would have been able to draw from tranche 1 in filling the role, and 35 percent from tranche 2. But on tranche 1, we can also look at how many of those players played a position that could have then shifted and covered for that spot. We'd need some eligibility criteria for all of this (probably a minimum number of games played) but it would just be a matter of multiplication. Shortstop would be harder to fill, and managers would probably be dipping a little further down in the talent pool, and so replacement level would be lower, as it is now.

Doing some quick analysis, I found that the difference in just batting linear weights (haven't even gotten into running or fielding) between tranche 1 and tranche 2 in 2019 was about 6.5 runs, prorated across 650 PA. Between tranche 1 and tranche 3, it's 10.8 runs. The ability to shift those plate appearances up the ladder has some real value.

This part is important. We can also give credit to starters for the positions that they showed an ability to play, even if they didn't play them (this is the guy fully capable of playing center, but who's in a corner because the team already has a good center fielder) because he allows a team to carry a player who hits like a left fielder to functionally be the team's backup center fielder. He facilitates that movement upward among the tranches. We can start to appreciate the difference between a left fielder who would never be able to hack it in center (and the compensatory move that his team would have to make) and the left fielder who could do it, but just didn't have to very often.

Past that, you can continue to use whatever hitting and fielding and running metrics you like to determine a player's value, but when we get down to constructing that baseline, I'd argue we need a better conceptual and mathematical framework. It's going to require some more #GoryMath than we're used to, but I'd argue it's a better conceptualization of the way that MLB actually plays the game in 2020. If…y'know…MLB plays in 2020. If WAR is going to be our flagship statistic among the *acronymati*, then we need to acknowledge that it contains some old and starting-to-be-out-of-date assumptions about the game. We may need to tinker with it. Here's my idea for how.

—*Russell A. Carleton is an author of Baseball Prospectus.*

Secondhand Sport

by Patrick Dubuque

Back before time stopped, I liked to go to thrift stores. Now that I'm older, I rarely ever buy anything—I don't need much in my life, now—but I still enjoy the old familiar circuit: check to see if there are baseball cards to write about, look for board or card games to play with the kids, scan for random ironic jerseys, hit the book section. It takes ten, maybe fifteen minutes. Thrift stores are the antithesis of modern online shopping, because you don't know what they have, and you don't even really know what you want. It's junk, literal junk, stuff other people thought was worthless. That's what makes it great.

In an idealized economy, thrift stores shouldn't exist. Everybody has a living wage, and every product has a durability that exactly matches its desired life; nothing should need to be given away, no one should need to be given to. But then, thrift stores shouldn't work on a customer experience level, either. You wouldn't think an ethos of "let's make everything disorganized and hard to find" would lead to customer satisfaction, but low-budget retailers like TJ Maxx and Ross thrive on this model. People like bargain hunting as much for the hunting as the bargain; it's part of the experience, spending time as if it's a wager. There's a thrill, occasionally, in inefficiency.

In sports, the modern overuse of the word "inefficiency" is a condemnation: It insinuates that there is *an* efficiency, a correct way to be found, and that all other ways are wrong ways. It's prevalent in baseball but hardly contained to it; the lifehack, the Silicon Valley disruption are other examples of productivity creep in our daily lives. Their modern success makes plenty of sense. Maximization of resources, after all, is its own puzzle, and an industry of European board games is founded upon it. It's fun to take a system and optimize it, unravel it like a sudoku puzzle. If there's only one kind of genius, after all, there's no way anyone can fail to appreciate it.

Baseball has been hacking away at these perceived inefficiencies since its inception: platoons, bullpens, farm systems were all installed to extract more out of the tools at hand. But it's been a particular badge of the sabermetric movement, from Ken Phelps and his All-Star Team to Ricardo Rincon and the darlings of *Moneyball*. It's business, but it's also an ethos: the idea that there's treasure among the trash, something we all failed to appreciate until someone brought it to light.

It's the myth that made Sidd Finch so enticing, that fuels so many "best shape" narratives and new pitch promises. We all, athletes and unathletic sportswriters, want to believe that there's genius trapped inside us, and that it's just a matter of puzzling out the combination to unlock it. That our art, our style is the next inefficiency, waiting for our own Billy Beane. It's why we root for underdogs, and why we're excited for the Mike Tauchmans and the Eurubiel Durazos, champions of skin-deep mediocrity.

Except we aren't anymore, really. The days of "Free X" have descended beyond the ring of irony and into obscurity. There are still Xs to be freed, or at least one X, duplicated endlessly: Mike Ford, Luke Voit, Max Muncy. The undervalued one-dimensional slugger demonstrated how the game hasn't quite culturally caught up to its logical extreme. But for those who don't fit the rather spacious mold, times are grimmer. As Rob Arthur revealed several months ago, there's been a marked increase in the number of sub-replacement relievers. It's the outcome of a greater number of teams forced to play out games without the talent to win them, but it's also emblematic of the modern tendency of teams to dispose of their disposable assets, burning through cost-controlled arms the way that man chopped down forests in *The Lorax*. Stuff just isn't built to outlive their original owners anymore.

It's unsurprising, given how well-mined the market for inefficiencies has been of late. The disciples of the early analytics departments, and the disciples of those, have proliferated the league, with only a few backwater holdouts. The league has grown smarter, but every team has learned the same lesson. In fact, the phenomenon creates a peculiar kind of feedback loop: As teams value a specific subset of players or skills, prospective athletes learn to increase their own marketability by conforming themselves to the demands of their prospective employers.

And that's tragic, in the way that the extinction of animals is tragic; a certain amount of biodiversity in baseball has been lost. Shortstops hit like outfielders. Pitchers don't hit at all. Only the catchers remain idiosyncratic, thanks to the defensive demands of their position; eventually they too will be required to produce like everyone else, or they'll meet the fate of their battery mates. A perfect economy requires perfect production.

I mentioned earlier that more and more, I leave thrift stores empty-handed. It is true that I am more discerning than in the past; my bookshelves are full, and there are more streaming films than I will ever be able to watch. But there are other factors at play.

Thrift stores are, in a way, the bond markets of retail. When the economy is rough and other retailers are struggling, more people look secondhand for their products. But as recently as last year, publications were noting a reversal of the trend: Companies like Goodwill and Savers were expanding despite a strong economy. Publications credited a heightened sense of environmentalism and a rejection of cutting-edge fashion as drivers behind the increase, though the more likely answer is the modern American economy hasn't showered its favors equally, particularly among the young.

But it is more than just the economy. Baseball and thrift stores share something else in common, evident in our current conversations about restarting the sport: They live in the gray area between public service and private enterprise. Thrift stores provide affordable necessities to lower-class citizens, and collectibles and fashion for the middle-class. Because of the success of the latter, prices have gone up across the board. Especially in terms of clothing, the middle-class flight from fashion into vintage has instead carried the aftereffects of fashion, including its costs, into a territory where people just want clothes. But there's another factor in the rise of prices, in the form of the internet.

The Goodwills of the world have grown smarter, too, employing the internet to extract full value from their detritus. Ebay, similarly, has lost much of the charm it had as a new frontier around the turn of the century. Everything has a price point now; even individual taste is no match for the algorithm, because anything rare, no matter how niche its market, is a collectible to someone.

The internet has had the same effect on thrift stores that sabermetrics has had on baseball; its equivalent to OBP was the bar scanner. As detailed in Slate, the rise of second-party stores on eBay and Amazon birthed an entire industry of used-good salespeople, armed with PDAs and scanners, buying books for three dollars to sell online for five. The author, Michael Savitz, reports earning $60,000 by working nearly 80 hours a week; he makes it clear that this is not a vocation of his choosing. It's long hours, with no real creativity or individuality, skimming the cream off of a local establishment and flipping it to someone with a little more money on the other side of the country. And once the vocation exists, the obvious question arises: why wait to put the wares out on the shelves? Why allow value to exist at all?

Nothing is ruined. Thrift stores will continue to sell polo shirts and DVDs, and baseball will continue to exist and make or lose money, depending on who you believe. But as we continue to refine our knowledge, we lose something in the conquest for efficiency, a delight born out of the unknown. The problem isn't the efficiency itself; we can't blame the booksellers, or the people sweeping freeways to collect grams of platinum from damaged catalytic converters. The problem is a system that requires this sort of profit-skimming behavior in order to feed families (or, for corporations, maximize shareholder return).

Los Angeles Angels 2021

In times like these, with the 2020 season on the brink and the collective bargaining agreement close behind, it can often feel like the current situation is untenable. It can't keep going like this, even if we don't know what to do about it. But as with thrift stores, there's an equally irresistible feeling that it *has* to keep going, that it would be unimaginable to not have this broken, amazing sport. Both industries exist on an invisible foundation of friction, of chaos and unpredictability, even as both see their foundations buffed down to a perfect, untouchable polish. But if COVID-19 and its financial ramifications do, as some have suggested, make it such that the baseball that returns is fundamentally different than the baseball that came before, perhaps this is the time to lean in, and change the game even more. Fix bunting. Make defense more difficult. Create viable, alternate strategies. Add some chaos back into baseball. It's fun when no one knows quite where things are.

—Patrick Dubuque is an author of Baseball Prospectus.

Steve Dalkowski Dreaming

by Steven Goldman

We dream of being a pitcher, of starring in the major leagues. Depending on your age and your sense of historical perspective, you might imagine yourself as Walter Johnson, throwing harder than anyone else—hitting more batters than anyone else, too, but always feeling bad about it. You could picture yourself as a Tom Seaver or a David Cone, with all the stuff in the world but still being cerebral about it, thinking about so much more than burning 'em in there. There are so many models one could choose: You could be a Lefty Gomez, Jim Bouton, or Bill Lee, skilled, but not taking the whole thing too seriously, or a Lefty Grove, Bob Gibson, or Steve Carlton, powerful but treating each start like a mission to be survived instead of a game to be enjoyed.

Very few would dream of being Steve Dalkowski, the former Baltimore Orioles prospect who died of COVID-19 last week at the age of 80. Yet, there is something just as noble in Dalkowski's negative accomplishments—and accomplishments is what they are—as there is in the precision-engineered pitching of a Greg Maddux. You have to be very good to be that bad. Dalkowski had all of the stuff of the greatest pitchers but none of the command; his story is not one of failing to conquer his limitations, but striving against one of the cruelest hands that fate or genetics or personality can deal us: A desire to achieve great things which is almost but not quite matched by the ability to meet that goal.

As with Johnson, Grove, Bob Feller, and the rest of the hard-throwing pitchers who played before the advent of modern radar guns, we have to take the word of the players and coaches who saw Dalkowski pitch as to his velocity. He was a hard-drinking, maximum-effort pitcher who, if their memories are to be believed, consistently threw over 100 miles per hour. His was the Maltese Fastball, the stuff that dreams are made of. The problem is that velocity without command and control is still a good distance from utility. Dalkowski was the most effective towel you could design for a fish, the sleekest bathing suit intended to be worn by an astronaut, but that doesn't mean he wasn't beautiful: We can appreciate a journey even if it doesn't end at the intended destination.

Whether because of sloppy mechanics he couldn't calm, an inability to understand that a consistent 98 in the strike zone would likely be more effective than a consistent 110 out of it, or all that beer, Dalkowski could never make the adjustments that pitchers like Feller and Nolan Ryan made before him, possibly because he had so far to go: Feller, who never pitched in the minors, came up at 17 and spent three years walking almost seven batters per nine innings before settling in at 3.8 beginning when he was 20. Ryan started out walking over six batters per nine but gradually improved as his long career played out; for him to go from 6.2 walks per nine with the 1966 Greenville Mets to 3.7 with the 1989 Texas Rangers represents a 40 percent reduction. An equivalent improvement by Dalkowski would still have left him walking over 11 batters per nine innings.

Dalkowski was like *The Room* of pitchers, a player so bad he became good again. Cal Ripken, Sr., who both played with and managed Dalkowski, recalled in a 1979 *Sporting News* "where are they now" piece the occasion when the pitcher crossed up his catcher and his fastball, "hit the plate umpire smack in the mask. The mask broke all to pieces and the umpire wound up in the hospital for three days with a concussion. If they ever had a radar gun in those days, I'll bet Dalkowski would have been timed at 110 miles an hour."

Signed by the Orioles out of New Britain High in Connecticut in 1957, Dalkowski was sent to Kingsport in the Appalachian League, where he pitched 62 innings. He allowed only 22 hits in 62 innings, or 3.2 per nine, a number with no equivalent in major league history (though Aroldis Chapman came close in 2014), and also struck out 121 (17.6 per nine) and walked 129 (18.7). He was also charged with 39 wild pitches. That June, one of his fastballs clipped a Dodgers prospect named Bob Beavers and carried away part of his ear. "The first pitch was over the backstop, the second pitch was called a strike, I didn't think it was," Beavers said last year. "The third pitch hit me and knocked me out, so I don't remember much after that. I couldn't get in the sun for a while, and I never did play baseball again." Former minor leaguer Ron Shelton based the *Bull Durham* pitcher Nuke LaLoosh on Dalkowski. And yet, to see him as a figure of fun, an amusing loser, is to misunderstand something unique and strange.

Dalkowski kept on posting some of the strangest lines in baseball history. Pitching for the Stockton Ports of the Class C California League in 1960, he struck out 262 and walked 262 in 170 innings. Yet, he did improve, especially after pitching for Earl Weaver at Elmira in 1962. Weaver had previously had Dalkowski at Aberdeen in 1959, but wasn't ready to grapple with him then. This time he was. "I had grown more and more concerned about players with great physical abilities who could not learn to correct certain basic deficiencies no matter how much you instructed or drilled them," he related in his autobiography, *It's What You Learn After You Know It All That Counts*. He got permission from the Orioles to give all of his players the Stanford-Binet IQ test. "Dalkowski finished in the 1 percentile in his ability to understand facts. Steve, it was said to say, had the ability to do everything but learn." [sic]

IQ tests are problematic diagnostic tools, so take Weaver's estimate of Dalkowski's mental capabilities with a grain of salt. What's important is that even if he got to the right answer by way of the wrong reason, Weaver had learned something valuable. His insight was to stop asking Dalkowski to learn new pitches and just let him get by with the two that he had. Were Dalkowski a prospect today, that would have been a no-brainer: Can't develop a third pitch? The bullpen is right over there, sir. Player development wasn't like that then, but Weaver, temporarily Dalkowski's mentor, could let him work with what he had. According to Weaver, the pitcher responded: "In the final 57 innings he pitched that season Dalkowski gave up 1 earned run, struck out 110 batters, and walked only 11." It's not true—as per the *Elmira Star-Gazette*, as of late July, Dalkowski had walked 71 in 106 innings and finished with 114 in 160 innings, which means Dalkowski's control actually faded at the end of the season rather than improved—but that doesn't mean it didn't happen in some sense, just that it didn't happen that way. Again, it's the journey, not the destination, and his ERA was 3.04 so *something* had gone right.

Also along the way: The next spring, Orioles manager Billy Hitchcock was rooting for Dalkowski to make the team as a long-man—maybe Weaver had gotten through to him. There were things out of Weaver's control, like the universe's twisted sense of humor: that March, Dalkowski's elbow went "twang."

You sometimes read that it was the Orioles' insistence on Dalkowski learning the curve that did him in, but even if they hadn't learned their lesson, the injury was probably just a coincidence: Dalkowski had thrown an incredible number of pitches over the previous few years. Still, it testifies to the dangers of trying to get what you want and risking the loss of what you had. Dalkowski tried to come back, but the 110-mph stuff was gone. A pitcher with no control and no stuff is…a civilian. What followed were years of vagabond living, arrests for drunkenness. There were Alcoholics Anonymous meetings, assistance from baseball alumni associations, but none of it took. From the 1990s until the time of his passing he dwelt in an assisted living facility, suffering from alcohol-related dementia. He'd been a heavy drinker since his teenage years. As with all those pitches per game, there was a price to be paid. You make choices on the journey and some of them are irrevocable. It's like a fairy tale: "Bite of poison apple? Don't mind if I do."

In the aforementioned *Sporting News* profile, Chuck Stevens, the head of the Association of Professional Ballplayers of America, a ballplayer charity, said, "I've got nothing against drinking. I do it myself sometimes. But, I don't condone common drunkenness. We went through lots of heartache and many dollars, but Dalkowski didn't want to help himself and we weren't going to keep him drunk." The journey is *un*like a fairy tale: No one will come along and kiss it better, not if they're busy forming judgments.

Los Angeles Angels 2021

In the end, we are left with a sort of philosophical chicken/egg conundrum: Is failing to meet your goals evidence of unfulfilled potential or the lack of it? Isn't what you did by definition what you were capable of doing? Or could you have broken through to something better with the right help, the right lucky break? These are unanswerable questions, and how we try to answer them may say more about us than about the people we're judging.

No pitcher ever has it easy. *All* pitchers must work hard. *All* pitchers must refine their craft. It's almost never just about *stuff*. Dalkowski dreaming is no insult to the great pitchers who made it; from Pete Alexander to Max Scherzer, they have all earned their way up. And yet, if it is true that we can only do as much as we can do, then the journey would be more of an adventure, the ultimate triumph or defeat more noble, if like Dalkowski we lacked 100 percent of the confidence, the command, the self-possession, the commitment, the resistance to making bad decisions that so many great players possess—to be gloriously human. Or, to put it more succinctly, it would be fun to be able to throw as hard as any person ever has. Even if just for a moment, and even if nothing more came of it than that, no one could say you hadn't lived life to the fullest.

—Steven Goldman is an author of Baseball Prospectus.

A Reward For A Functioning Society

by Cory Frontin and Craig Goldstein

On July 5, Nationals reliever Sean Doolittle said in the middle of a press conference regarding the restart of Major League Baseball and what would later be known as summer camp, "sports are like the reward of a functioning society." This sentence was amidst a much longer, thoughtful reply about the societal and health conditions under which MLB players were being brought back. It's a very similar sentiment to one Jane McManus used on April 7, when she discussed the White House's meeting with sports commissioners. She said "sports are the effect of a functioning society—not the precursor."

Both versions of the same sentiment spoke to a laudable ideal in the context of a country that was not addressing a rampaging virus, and opting instead to bring sports back for the feeling of normalcy rather than the reality of it. "Priorities," as McManus said.

On Wednesday, the NBA's Milwaukee Bucks conducted a wildcat/political strike, refusing to come out for Game 5 of their playoff series against the Orlando Magic. The Magic refused to accept the forfeit, and shortly thereafter other playoff series were threatened by player strikes. Eventually the league moved to postpone that day's games, folding to players leveraging their united power.

The backdrop against which these actions took place was the shooting by police of Jacob Blake. Blake was shot in the back seven times by police, as he attempted to get into his vehicle. He managed to survive the assault, but is paralyzed from the waist down.

⚾ ⚾ ⚾

The step taken to walk out, first by the Milwaukee Bucks, then subsequently by other NBA, WNBA, and MLB teams, was a step toward upholding the virtue of the sentiment described by McManus and Doolittle. But that sentiment does not align with the broad history of sports in this and other countries, a history that contradicts the core of the idealistic statement.

Sports have been a significant part of American society for most of its existence, expanding in importance and influence in recent years. The idea that society was functioning in a way that was worthy of the reward of sports for most of that time is laughable. Much of America is not functioning and has not functioned for Black people, full stop. The oppressed people at the center of this political act by players, specifically Black players, in concert throughout the NBA and in fits and starts throughout Major League Baseball, have not known a society that functions for them rather than *because* of them.

Politics has been part of the sports landscape since the inception of sport, but for just about as long people have bemoaned its presence. Sports are to be an escape, it is said. An escape from what, though? A functioning society?

No, the presence of sports has never signified a cultural or political system that is on the up and up. Rather, the presence of sports *reflect and reinforce the society* that produces them.

⚾ ⚾ ⚾

The Negro Leagues were born out of societal dysfunction. The need for entirely separate leagues, composed of Black and Latino players barred from the Major Leagues because of racism? That is not a functioning society, and yet there were sports.

Even the integration of players from the Negro Leagues resulted in a transfer of power and wealth from Black-owned businesses and communities and into white ones, mirroring the dysfunction that had bled into every aspect of American society at the time. Japheth Knopp noted in the Spring 2016 Baseball Research Journal:

> The manner in which integration in baseball—and in American businesses generally—occurred was not the only model which was possible. It was likely not even the best approach available, but rather served the needs of those in already privileged positions who were able to control not only the manner in which desegregation occurred, but the public perception of it as well in order to exploit the situation for financial gain. Indeed, the very word integration may not be the most applicable in this context because what actually transpired was not so much the fair and equitable combination of two subcultures into one equal and more homogenous group, but rather the reluctant allowance—under certain preconditions—for African Americans to be assimilated into white society.

To understand the value of a movement, though, is not to understand how it is co-opted by ownership, but to know the people it brings together and what they demand. When Jackie Robinson—the player who demarcated the inevitability of the end of the Negro leagues—attended the March on Washington for Jobs and Freedom in 1963, he did so with his family and marched alongside the people. He stood alongside hundreds of thousands to fight for their common civil and labor rights. "The moral arc of the universe is long," many freedom fighters have echoed, "but it bends towards justice." The bend, it is less frequently said, happens when a great mass of people place the moral arc of the universe on their knee and apply force, as Jackie, his family, and thousands of others did that day.

⚾ ⚾ ⚾

Of course, taking the moral arc of the universe down from the mantle and bending it is not without risk. Perhaps the outsized influence of athletes is itself a mark of a dysfunctional society, but, nonetheless, hundreds of athletes woke up on Wednesday morning with the power to bring in millions of dollars in revenues. That very power, as we would come to find out, was matched with the equal and opposite power to *not* bring those revenues. That power, in hands ranging from the Milwaukee Bucks, to Kenny Smith in the *Inside the NBA* Studio, from the unexpected ally, Josh Hader, and his largely white teammates to the notably Black Seattle Mariners, would be exercised for a single demand: the end to state violence against Black people. Not unlike the March itself, it sat at the intersection of the civil rights of Black Americans and bold labor action. The March on Washington stood in the face of a false notion of integration—against an integration of extraction but not one of equality—and proposed something different. Just the same, the acts of solidarity of August 26, 2020 will be remembered in stark defiance of MLB's BLM-branded, but ultimately empty displays on opening weekend.

Bold defiance like this can never be without risk. By choosing to exercise this power, the Milwaukee Bucks took a risk. They risked vitriol and backlash from those they disagreed with. They risked fines or seeing their contracts voided, as a walkout like this is prohibited by their CBA. They risked forfeiting a playoff game, one that, as the No. 1 seed in the playoffs, they'd worked all year to attain. They didn't know how Orlando would respond. It wasn't clear that other teams throughout the league would follow suit in solidarity. And it wasn't known the league would accept these actions and moderately co-opt them by "postponing" games that would have featured no players.

If the league reschedules the games, some of the athletes' risk—their shared sacrifice—will be diminished, in retrospect. But they did not know any of that when they took that risk. And it is often left to athletes to take these risks when others in society won't, especially those of their same socioeconomic status and levels of influence.

It is athletes, specifically BIPOC athletes, that take them, though, because they live with the risk of being something other than white in this country every day. They are no strangers to the realities of police brutality. It seems incongruous then, to say that sports are a reward for a functioning society when we rely on athletes to lead us closer to being a functioning society. Luckily, our beloved athletes, WNBA players first and foremost among them, understand what sports truly are: a pipebender for the moral arc of the universe.

—*Craig Goldstein is editor in chief of Baseball Prospectus. Cory Frontin is an author of Baseball Prospectus.*

Index of Names

Adams, Jordyn	75, 92		Marsh, Brandon	81, 91
Adell, Jo	16		Martinez, Orlando	82, 96
Bard, Luke	84		Mayers, Mike	65
Barreto, Franklin	76		Naughton, Packy	86
Barria, Jaime	47		Ohtani, Shohei	27
Blakely, Werner	97		Ortega, Oliver	86
Bundy, Dylan	49		Paris, Kyren	82, 93
Buttrey, Ty	51		Peña, Felix	67
Canning, Griffin	53		Placencia, Adrian	97
Claudio, Alex	55		Pujols, Albert	29
Cobb, Alex	57		Quijada, José	87
Detmers, Reid	85, 92		Quintana, José	88
Fernandez, Jose Miguel	77		Rendon, Anthony	31
Fletcher, David	19		Rengifo, Luis	33
Fowler, Dexter	21		Rivera, Jose	98
García, Robel	77		Rodriguez, Chris	88, 94
Gosselin, Phil	23		Sandoval, Patrick	69
Guerra, Junior	59		Slegers, Aaron	71
Heaney, Andrew	61		Stassi, Max	35
Hernandez, Aaron	85		Suarez, José	89
Iglesias, José	25		Suzuki, Kurt	37
Iglesias, Raisel	63		Teheran, Julio	73
Jackson, Jeremiah	78, 94		Thaiss, Matt	83
Jones, Jahmai	98		Trout, Mike	39
Knowles, D'Shawn	79, 95		Upton, Justin	41
Kochanowicz, Jack	96		Walsh, Jared	43
Lagares, Juan	79		Ward, Taylor	45
Maitan, Kevin	80		Yan, Hector	98

For the Joy of Keeping Score

THIRTY81 Project is an ongoing graphic design project focused on the ballparks of baseball. Since being established in 2013, scorecards have been a fundemantal part of the effort. Each two-page card is uniquely ballpark-centric — there are 30 variants — and designed with both beginning and veteran scorekeepers in mind. Evolving over the years with suggestions from fans, broadcasters, and official scorers, the sheets are freely available to everyone as printable letter-size PDFs at the project webshop: www.THIRTY81Project.com

Download, Print, Score, Repeat ...

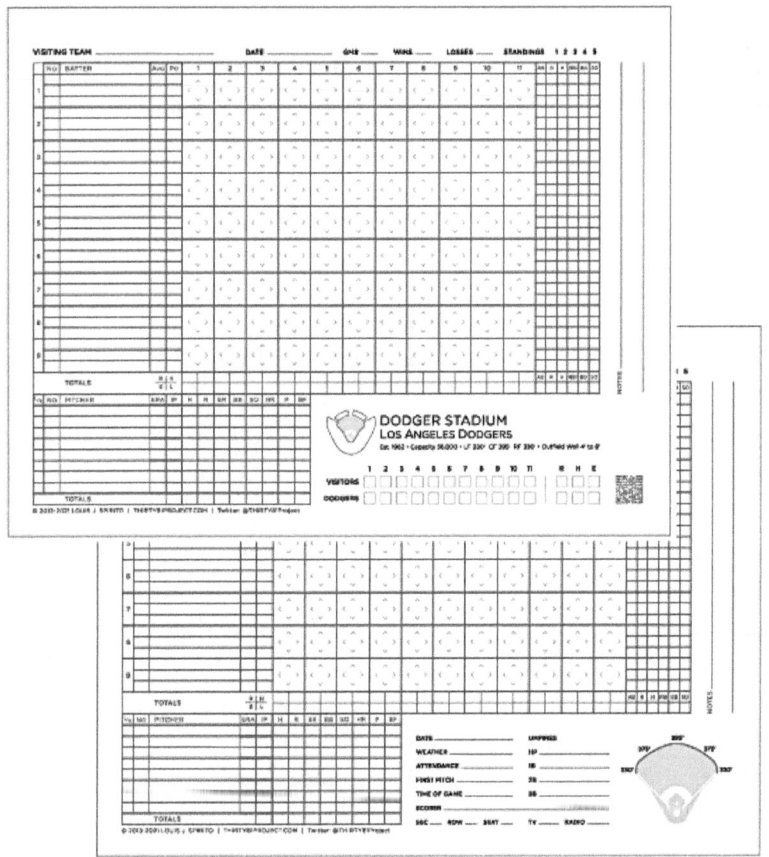

Scorecard design ©2013-2021 Louis J. Spirito | THIRTY81Project